This copy of *Feasting On Sales Crumbs*

is presented to:

_____

I believe in your gifts and talents and stand in agreement
for your *complete success* - Mentally, Spiritually, Socially,
Physically, and Financially.

By:

_____

Brandon Clay Enterprises, LLC

THE SALES CRUMBS
TRILOGY VOLUME III

Feasting On Sales Crumbs

A Guide to Achieving Sales Success &
Life Mastery

Focusing On Things That Bring Sales Success and Life Fulfillment

Brandon L. Clay

This publication is designed to provide accurate and authoritative information in regard to the subject matter covered. It is sold with the understanding that the publisher and author are not engaged in rendering legal, accounting, or other professional services. If legal advice or other expert assistance is required, the services of a competent professional should be sought.

Published by Brandon Clay Enterprises, LLC
McDonough, GA
www.brandonlclay.com

Distributed by Brandon Clay Enterprises, LLC.

For ordering information or special discounts for bulk purchases, please email Brandon Clay Enterprises, LLC at orders@brandonlclay.com

Design and composition by Brandon Clay Enterprises, LLC
Cover Design by Brandon Clay Enterprises, LLC

1st Edition

This work and *everything* I do is dedicated to my best friend and wife, Natalie. All my love and devotion!

To the millions of people, worldwide, who are pursuing greatness that may happen upon one of my works: I believe in the nobility of sales and your ability to be a top professional.   My greatest desire is that something said within these pages will impact your life and set you on course to unleash all the greatness that is within you!

I wish you Money, Power, and Success!

Table of Contents

Author's Preface

Emotions fill my heart and mind as you begin the process of reading this last volume in the Sales Crumbs Trilogy. I am filled with great reward and satisfaction that you have come this far on the voyage of discovery, and that I have been able to be a part of that journey. This final Volume - **Feasting on Sales Crumbs** is a rapid-fire rocket-ride into the activities that encompass the life of a successful sales professional. *Throughout the trilogy, I have relayed how sales is a form of sharing.* All of life is about *giving to receive* - connectedness that requires we give what we have to get what we need/desire. If you will allow me to wax poetic, and I will be brief, there are a myriad of ways to share;

Share experiences - *Can you remember your first sale?* Would you be willing to share that momentous occasion with someone that is just getting into your industry? Those 5 minutes may be what it takes to get them through a nervous time.

Share moments - Do you go home and grumble "It's over" when your spouse or kids ask how the day went? I was that way once - I realized that my energy made my wife and kids "*hate my job on my behalf*". I then began to share the high level "goods and not so goods" in story form. They got to know my colleagues through my stories and were truly interested. They then began to "root" for me and my performance improved...*sharing was an important part of that success!*

  Share concerns and fears - You need an outlet for the things that concern you and the fears that might stall you. Be certain, sharing concerns and fears makes you *highly vulnerable* - be judicious and discriminating with whom you share your "kryptonite weaknesses"...*but take heart...*<u>we ALL have something we struggle with!</u> Sharing at this level is cathartic and cleansing - *sometimes all we need is to say what is on our mind to get rid of it!*

  Share success - Many of us shirk the spotlight of achievement in a sense of false humility. Arrogance is not the answer either, but we should provide a "living testimony" to someone who is looking for a sign that *success is possible for them.* Sharing success means divulging elements of the dark, painful side of what you went through and the price you paid. Be willing to share your prize winning roses, but also let people see your thorn scarred hands!

  <u>Sharing is the real secret of success</u>. *It allows people to get involved in your life.* It relays to them the things you love, the things you fear, and the things you desire. In your life, you will only pursue *with passion* those things that <u>attract you.</u> Real attraction doesn't require nudging or nurturing - you are compelled to pursue it relentlessly...like a magnet draws iron. Attraction gives birth to desire and desire starts you on your

way - the process of completion has begun. *As you share with others, there will be people sent to help you walk out your destiny.*

Understand that your Evolution to Completion is a process. Energy expended for development is the price that must be paid for progress within that process. *Attempting anything requires energy.* The attempt may not immediately result in the desired outcome, but that "failure" is temporary if energy is renewed and second and third (ad infinitum - meaning never give up!) attempts are made in a new, evolving way. This process of Getting Better through continued attempts is the cornerstone of achievement. New opportunities will take you out of your comfort zone. That means doing *what you do* (sharing) in front of people who <u>may not clap</u> when you are finished - that is the risk of exposure. What is the reward for that risk - the possibility of a standing ovation!!!

"*Life is not a dress rehearsal*" - **Rose Tremain**.

As you travel to the next level of success**, <u>enjoy the journey</u>**. We have been given <u>one life</u> to live, enjoy, and express our greatest gifts and talents. Somehow on that road to expression, we get more caught up in "the end" than "the middle". As I typed these words, I can't help but see the audiences, the people impacted, and sitting next to Oprah. Then something subtle strikes my spirit and I am pulled back into *the now* - the attractiveness of my home, the power of the song playing in the background, the magical way words are filling in a once blank page - *by my hand...by my mind...***all given to me by God**. The tears begin to flow because this is *my middle - my journey. This is my highest form of sharing.* What part will you play in this thing called life?

"All the world's a stage, and all the men and women merely players: they have their exits and their entrances; and one man in his time plays many parts, his acts being seven ages" - **William Shakespeare.**

The day you were born the curtain was pulled back. All of us will eventually have a "curtain call" in our lives when we are recognized for *being special* - impacting an individual (like a child), a group, or being instrumental in a global movement. *The magnitude is not important.* It is what you do in-between that matters most...*living out your play.* **Live your life with purpose and passion**. _Serve those you are called to impact, receive the reward of that service but most of all...enjoy!_ Make no mistake that you, just like Matt, are on the sure road to success if you employ the concepts outlined in this series. Of this I have no doubt - if you share the best of who you are. I will leave you to enjoy your road but as is my custom, **I wish you Money, Power, and Success!**

And now, Volume III of the Sales Crumbs Trilogy...

Act I - Selling Out to Sales

You've Got Mail!

Happy Monday! Matt said enthusiastically to the early risers that were already in the office. He had arrived at 7:30am just as he had declared in his Get Better session with Jack Jeffries a week earlier. The usual people were there; Larry, the sales manager and some of the administrative team. As he sat down in his chair at the table, there was a note - "You've got mail".

To keep the newbies from wasting precious time on the computer with email and senseless surfing, they weren't given a computer until they graduated from the Fast Start training program. It wasn't a big deal since Matt knew that people did use these things as an excuse to keep from doing the *real work*. He had only gotten a few emails anyway.

He went to the community computer and pulled up his email. It was from his sister-in-law Lori, the National Sales Director for a fortune 50 healthcare company. Matt remembered that she was going to send him and Tim an outline for professional sales development after their debate. He liked the things that she had said at the cookout and felt he could benefit from her experience. The subject of the email read: **The E^4 Sales Success Roadmap.** Matt liked the sound of that and began to read the email;

Good morning Tim and Matt,

The last few days I have given a lot of thought to our robust discussion on helping sales people progress through the four phases - Lead Junkie, Order Taker, and Professional culminating in a thriving career as a Trusted Advisor. Ultimately, it comes down to two key things -**The People and The Process**.

- **People** - Sales people have to possess the two basic raw materials that can be developed into higher levels of sales achievement. These are *energy* and *ethics*. This combination generates self-motivation to control their *own destiny* - one that does not require artificial stimulus through "carrots or sticks". When properly indentified and leveraged in the recruiting process, this combination will instill the necessary traits of dogged persistence, a desire for product excellence, and a customer centric approach that builds strong relationships.

- **Process** - This is the strategic outline that guides sales people through the 4 stages. It is scalable to provide a template for small, large, national and multi-national sales organizations. It is also *customizable* to account for market dynamics and/or the individual learning styles of the sales people. This template is dynamic and not cookie cutter. It will identify strengths and weaknesses at an individual level and maximize strengths while compensating for weaknesses - so you don't lose otherwise good people needlessly.

Tim, I can hear your thoughts! Yes, if a person's weaknesses present major stumbling blocks, then <u>hard choices</u> have to be made - choices of *who can be developed and others that may not make it on our teams.* **The development process is not a smoke screen for those sales people that just aren't cut out for the profession or industry.** These hard decisions can be made in a way that preserves the dignity of the fallen and the morale of the remaining team members who secretly wonder "*if I am next?*".

The E^4 Sales Success Roadmap has 4 core elements that determine proper development of a sales person;

1. <u>Evaluate</u> - The power of the evaluation stage is that it uncovers strengths, reveals areas for improvement, development opportunities for weaknesses and opens your eyes to opportunity. It encompasses assessment of Product Knowledge, Sales Effectiveness from Prospecting models to Closing (Sales).

2. <u>Evolve</u> - After proper evaluation, some amount of evolution is usually necessary. Evolution adjusts to the environments and does not wait for conditions to improve. **It makes it happen!** It creates a compelling plan that maximizes strengths and compensates for weaknesses uncovered in the

Evaluate Phase. It brings them together to leverage opportunities.

3. **Expand** - Once a strong foundation is established, it is time to "build up". Playing to the uncovered strengths and high yield opportunities (the ones that are most likely to bring positive results) you generate higher levels of *effective activity*.

4. **Explode** - To continue the building analogy, once a skyscraper has a proper foundation (Evaluate and Evolve) and the scaffolding is in place (Expand) the edifice goes up quickly. The resulting template from the first 3 phases is the "secret formula" that can be utilized to generate tremendous results - *to explode your business!*

Attached you will find four PDF's that take you through an E^4 Boot Camp. *It is a review of where you are today and provides a roadmap to improvement and development.* They contain a rapid fire series of actions and activities that are best reviewed in a "brainstorm" environment with buy in from sales leadership and dedicated members of the sales team. I hope this information is helpful...call me if you want to discuss further. *Continued success to both of you!*

Lori Thompson, National Sales Director.

Matt opened the attached files and was surprised at the simple layout. Seeing it laid out this way confirmed that what he had been learning *was* pointing him in the right direction. This roadmap would be the key to faster progression. His mind was reeling from all that Lori outlined - *a process that he could follow and be successful.* <u>He also realized he could not do it alone</u>. As the Table of 4 came in, he showed them the email. They all had the same reaction.

"With this as a process and platform, we could accelerate our success," said Suzy excitedly.

"This is the type of desktop procedure approach we used in operations," added David. "It benchmarked our progress and success in a quantitative and qualitative way. I work best in a measured environment - this is terrific!"

"They *are* measuring us...by our sales, *right?*" said Brad who was struggling to see the bigger picture.

Matt spoke up first, "Yes, but right now, if our sales are our *only* judge -"

"The number of sales will eventually be our *only jury*," said David.

"How would the three of you feel if we could enact what Lori has outlined?" Matt asked.

"Great!" they said in unison.

"Then I am going to the sales manager with this."

Won't he be insulted? Isn't that kind of *his job* to take us through his process?" offered Brad with an uncharacteristic sensitivity.

"Yes, but on some level, he is like my brother-in-law Tom. The old school approach created by having *his neck* on the line based on the results of his team, *his own production*, and then having to take on 10 new recruits each 8 weeks makes it hard for him to provide us with what we need. Jack Jeffries said that the company owes us 'access to success' but that innovation, ingenuity and imagination is our part."

"I actually think he will be receptive," said David.

"*Or relieved*," concluded Suzy.

"In either event, I am going to see him now. Wish me luck!"

No "I" in team...but there is "ME"!

During lunchtime when Matt usually sits with the sales manager to do a 30 minute call review, he shows him the email from Lori. The sales manager is impressed. "This is a terrific philosophy and roadmap that she has outlined here and it looks to be very effective. While simple, it is thorough - a guide to help create the core template of sales success. Once your foundation is solid, it sets the stage for expanding your efforts - making it scalable. That said...*I am not sure what you want me to do with this?*"

"I am not sure either," began Matt, "I guess I wanted to see how we could adopt this process. To help those of us just getting started in sales, or those that have been here a while but are struggling."

"Yes, just making the cut and graduating from the Fast Start training program are no guarantees. I feel for the people who are sincerely making an effort, but their results don't bear that out. I make myself available to them but in some ways I am not in a position to give them what they need most - *individual attention*," he lamented.

Matt realized that the sales manager was facing his own pressures and regardless of his intentions, the deck was stacked against him. As making quota was the only thing that mattered, he was singularly focused on meeting it, and not people development. At least he was nicer than Tom in chastising the team when they fell short. He was also willing to his forgo lunch to sit with Matt every day. *He truly was doing the best he could.*

"Understand, showing you this is not an indictment of you or the company. I want to succeed and have been fortunate to have some good people mentor me," Matt reassured him knowing it was uncomfortable to hear he may not be doing enough for his team.

"*Like LeRoy?*" said the sales manager. "He is a good man that always tried to help me see the bigger picture. He preached that if I could spend more time developing and coaching I would eventually build a team that would blow past quota. I agreed with him, but it is -"

"Hard to coach when you have *to play*," finished Matt.

"That is not an excuse I will make, but our current process does leave much to be desired. The 10-day Fast Start training does a good job of establishing an initial foundation but does a poor job of *building on it.* I know that the best learning comes from doing. He pointed to a plaque on his desk. It was a quote from Confucius.

> *"I hear and forget. I see and I remember. I do and I understand."*

"Most of what we teach in that 10-day program is forgotten. Then as the newbies begin *to do*, and the learnings dissipate, they begin to 'wing' it. Then trial and error becomes their teacher - it becomes what they 'understand'. What they need is a mentor, like LeRoy, or a coach that can provide a watchful eye so bad habits don't become the norm."

"Like becoming and remaining a Lead Junkie," said Matt pointing to the email from Lori.

"Exactly! We want and need to foster an entrepreneurial environment, where people can call most of their own shots - run their own business. Reality is, not everyone is capable of running a business *without guidance*. I think of a friend who is a great dentist, but he is a poor businessman. In dentistry school they taught him the dentistry craft but did not develop his business acumen. As a result, his business struggles. That is what I see here...talented people who need *more guidance*. What is worse; they see their temporary base salary as a countdown to Armageddon."

"No joke - T-minus and counting for me!" Matt actually knew the day and hour when it would end.

"I understand that the base salary is a major plus and that most companies don't provide it. As a differentiator, it helps us recruit the *best talent* and take some of the angst of career transition away. If we could somehow leverage the *entire* guarantee period to do pure people development, without the pressure of quotas, those 3 months would be plenty of time to cultivate the core qualities of a sales professional."

Matt could only shake his head in agreement. He knew that some of the newbies were waiting out the 3 months and would then look for another job. Essentially collecting it like unemployment benefits.

"Look Matt, I know that many of the newbies see the base salary as a safety net and will leave after they have milked the cow for three months. *That can't be profitable for the company to invest so heavily just to have your investment walk out at ROI time.* Others see the countdown as a -"

"*A noose that constricts performance,*" admitted Matt.

"Sad but true. *Back to this plan* - I can't formally advocate this as something the company is behind but since it is general sales and business development material and not proprietary to another company, you are free to use it."

"I want to share it with my team if you don't mind."

"I see that the four of you are working hard, teaming and trying to support each other. I think that is great and don't believe it isn't noticed. Even Larry said something to the VP today about the effort and particularly, *your leadership.* He also mentioned your dinner the other day - *he was impressed!*"

"Yes, the Evan's Agency opportunity is a good one - though yet to materialize. I want to be able to leverage *every* opportunity and help my colleagues when possible. I know that sales is an individual sport, but I like connecting and teaming with my colleagues who can relate and provide me good feedback."

"In some ways you *are* coaching...*each other.* I am here for you and will do what I can," the sales manager said compassionately.

"Do you mind if we meet for the next three days to conduct an E^4 Boot Camp using this material?"

"Not at all, in fact, you can use the small conference room. There is a whiteboard, an easel with paper and a coffee pot. Have at it! While you are making me look good, I have to ask...you aren't gunning for my job *are you*?"

"Not just yet...let me get my second sale and get back with you!" both laughing. Inwardly, Matt did think of the changes he would make if he had the authority. As Matt went back to the table, he gave the thumbs up to the team.

"It went well?" asked David.

"Yes, he really is a nice guy with good intentions - just over matched based on company expectations and the current recruitment and training process."

"You know the saying?" said Suzy, "'the road to trouble is paved with good intentions'!"

"I told him we were going to do a four day E^4 Boot Camp to create our roadmap. We can start each day at 8:00am."

"There is a lot to cover, let's make it 7:30am," said Brad with a newfound energy.

"The eligible bachelor has spoken! If he can abstain from the 2am last call for alcohol at the local sports bar then we can all be here at 7:30am," said Suzy playfully.

"Then it's a plan!" said Matt triumphantly.

E⁴ Boot Camp - Day #1

Matt actually arrived at 6:30am to put together the materials for everyone for the day. It was quite a bit of material and there was a lot to read with several exercises to complete. He could feel that this work was important and would help him build a stronger foundation for his future. As he glanced over the material, much of it was familiar in concept, but now it was going to be "drilled in". He hoped the others were as excited as he was. He didn't have to wait long as the three of them arrived together at 7:15am.

"Good morning guys," Matt said with a burst of energy despite the early start.

"Good morning for sure," said David, "I am about to explode from anticipation of what the next four days will hold."

"Wow, there is a lot here!" commented Brad flipping through the clipped packet.

"If I understand this right, we are about to design *our lives*. It should be more than a cursory exercise and one that we should take very seriously," Suzy added.

"No doubt about that. This is important stuff and I am excited to get started," Matt echoing the sentiments of the group. "Notice the board and the packets I have prepared. Today we will focus on Evaluation. I thought maybe we could take turns leading the sessions by reading the section briefs and then completing the exercises - if that sounds good to you guys?"

"You are a natural born leader, Matt, and we're all fine doing this your way," confirmed David speaking for the others who were in agreement.

"Then I will begin," Matt standing in front of the room, began to read the material;

Day #1 Evaluate - the power of perspective. Sales can be complicated. There are so many things to do and be proficient in - prospecting, products, selling, closing, administration, servicing, and self-development. Looking at things universally can be overwhelming. *You must narrow your focus and concentrate.* The closer you look, the more you will see...the more you see, the more you understand...the more you understand, the more power you have – power that will turn into ability and higher sales. As you look deeper you will gain insight to;

o *Determine your strengths* - what activities are you strongest in and naturally gravitate to? Which prospecting methods yield the best closing rates? The key to rapid development is to play to your highest and best gifts. Evaluation will help you determine where you are strongest.

o *Uncover your weaknesses* - what are the areas of deficiency that are impacting your current performance? Do you avoid certain products due to their complexity? Is your close rate for a particular type of lead too low? There are some weaknesses that you can "outsource" to a resource that provides the needed competency. Are there other areas of weakness that will require development to achieve an acceptable level of performance? Evaluation will help you determine where you need that improvement or assistance.

o *Discover optimal opportunities* - as you evaluate your activities and their effectiveness, the highest yield opportunities will emerge from the review. This inspection will reveal the activities you should focus on to increase sales effectiveness. You will still integrate other areas that require development, but the majority of time should be spent where your "seeds of energy can provide a great harvest" and not spinning wheels in areas of low yield.

Evaluation is about determining where your business is today. Even if you are working for a Fortune 50 company with thousands of sales people or if you are a Lone Ranger - *you are running a business*. You must get out of the producer mindset and become a business person - *focused on being highly effective, driving new opportunity, and taking P & L (Profit and Loss) responsibility for all your efforts*. As the CEO of your company, there are some big picture questions you have to review;

o **Revenue analysis** - Sales people generate revenue in the form of salary and commissions - first year and renewals. List the revenue you have generated in the last three years (include other sales positions if less than three years with current company).

- Is your revenue increasing, decreasing or flat?

○ **Product focus** - If you offer a family of products, list how many sales you had in the previous 12 month period by product.

- Are the products you sell *the most* the ones that you are most comfortable with based on features, price, or other factors?
- Are the products you sell *the least* more complicated or more expensive?
- What products do you avoid totally? *Why?*

○ **Cross-Selling** - If you have a portfolio of products, cross-selling or getting repeat business is vital to your businesses' growth. How many products do you average per client?

- 1 product is symptomatic of an order taker.
- 2-3 products presents you as a professional to your clients.
- Full portfolio approach to clients establishes you as their trusted advisor.

o **Revenue by product** - to determine the highest yield opportunities, review the products sold and the revenue generated.

- By the list of products sold, calculate the total revenue (commission) generated.

- Does the product you sell the most generate the highest commission on a *per sale basis*?

- Do the products you sell the least have the *highest revenue potential?*

o **Lead generation** - Leads are the life's blood of your business. They are powerful for building momentum to *get you in motion*. As Newton's law states, once you are in motion, you should stay in motion! Evaluate the channels where your business comes from;

- Overall lead mix - in the last 12 months (and by month) identify where your leads came from - list number of telemarketing (direct efforts vs. outsourcing), direct mail, pre-set appointments, networking, referrals, repeat business, and other sources.

o **Close rates** - *Your sales effectiveness is governed by your ability to close sales.* If lead cost is inexpensive then the close rate can be lower, but if lead is expensive, close rates have to be higher. Let's evaluate;

- Overall close rate - take the total number of sales generated from all products and divide it by the total number of leads from all channels for last 12 months (and by month). *Is your close rate increasing by month? Does it dip when you add new products to your offerings?*

▪ <u>Close rate by channel</u> - how many sales did you get from each lead source? Take the number of sales attributable to a lead type (for example direct mail) and divide it by the total number of leads from that channel. *Does your close rate put you "in the pack" of your colleagues? Is one channel overwhelmingly stronger/weaker than others?* Does the close rate support the cost of generating the lead?

○ **<u>Summary</u>** - To get the highest and best use of your time, energy and resources, you need to rank your top 3 results for the past 12 months;

✓ What are your top 3 products sold?
✓ What are your top 3 products by revenue?
✓ What are your top 3 lead sources by volume?
✓ What are your top 3 lead sources by close rate?

This concludes Day One

"Whew! That was quite the exercise!" said Matt.

"I keep meticulous records, but I *never* evaluated my results this thoroughly," admitted Suzy.

"Anyone care to share what they discovered through this exercise?" Matt asked wanting someone else to go first.

"The first thing I noticed is that <u>all</u> my sales are the same product," began Brad, "I also calculated that my close rate isn't as good as I thought. Being #2 on the leaderboard of the newbies gave me the false sense of security that I was actually effective, but a 30% close rate says differently."

"Well, *I am #1* and I have had several revelations; First, I do well with the leads I generate from my own calls, closing 65%, but the leads from the call center I only close 40%. Second, I am averaging 2 products per client, which is good. However, we offer a product that combines those two products that is less expensive for the client and actually *pays more commission*."

"Why aren't you selling that one?" asked David. "It is a great product for the client," his operations background coming through.

"It is more complicated to explain and I have not built confidence with it yet," she confessed.

"I can help you with that...I know that product like the back of my hand! In fact, that is the product I need to present at my meetings next week," David said excitedly.

"Looks like we all learned some important lessons from evaluating our businesses," Matt remarked.

"I like the sound of that...*our businesses!*" interjected David feeling a new sense of ownership and opportunity.

"From this day forward, we are all CEO's," said Brad.

"Yes, Chief Evaluating Officers!" laughed Suzy.

"Tomorrow, we do the Evolve portion of the boot camp and I can't wait...see you guys tomorrow". Matt had a feeling of accomplishment and anticipation for what the next day would hold.

E⁴ Boot Camp - Day #2

It was 7:30am and the group assembled like clockwork to begin the day's boot camp review and exercises. Brad went up to the whiteboard to write down the discussion points, brainstorming elements, and to create a parking lot for things they needed outside help with. David went to the front of the room to begin reading the content for the day;

Day #2 Evolve - *The power of evolution is about where you want your business to be tomorrow.* It takes the facts uncovered in the Evaluate review and creates gradual and progressive change to an advanced level. It is designed to inspire and motivate to higher activity, effectiveness, and commitment to excellence. Leveraging the things learned through Evaluation you will;

o *Create a compelling future* - The best performance stimulus comes from visualizing the results of your efforts *before* you begin. Companies forecast their revenue at the beginning of each year and then build strategic plans to achieve them. You have to do the same. The sales profession is unique in that it allows you to "preset" your financial targets...your revenue. Companies set stretch goals as investors look for year over year revenue growth to validate their investment and generate a return. To Evolve, you need to elevate your mind and consider a higher revenue proposition.

▪ Take your last 12 months revenue from the Evaluation review. *Double it for next 12 months and that is your targeted revenue.*

▪ Before you begin a tactical review (covered in the Expand portion) how would this increase impact your professional and personal life? *Would you buy a nicer home or car? Would you send your kids to the best schools? Would you help your parents or give to a cause you are passionate about?* Remember the concept of Archimedic Leverage and understand that "why" achieving this target is important to create the proper motivation.

▪ Doubling your revenue for the next twelve months *is possible...*take a minute to let that soak in!!! As you ponder, there are three "reality" questions you need to ask;

> *Does your industry (and company) allow you to earn the desired amount? Is anyone in this industry (or company) earning this amount?* The final and most important question - *If it can be done and is being done...WHY NOT ME?*

▪ The key to generating more revenue is to create *more value* by helping *more people* solve their problems or achieve their desires for their lives. "*Strive not to be a success, but rather to be of value*" - **Albert Einstein.** As you serve...you deserve.

○ **Barriers to Evolution** - Mentally, you may be battling with your inability to generate the double revenue from increasing your effectiveness and evolving in the areas required to demonstrate this level of success. Before you can evolve your approach, you need to review what has stopped you in the past;

- *Lazy or satisfied* (Red Light) - These twin towers of mediocrity are what limit the vast majority of sales people. They are either too lazy to commit to the effort necessary to evolve, or they are content with the level of revenue they are currently demonstrating. At the core, both are suffering from a lack of proper motivation to spur increased production. Common symptoms;

- Your goals are not compelling enough - create a series of goals (what) and visualize the impact of reaching them (why). "*People are not lazy, they simply have impotent goals that do not inspire them*" - **Anthony Robbins**

- You focus only on yourself and not others - who else are you impacting with your performance (or lack of it!)? If you keep skipping the gym and your health fails, who will suffer the consequences *besides you?* As humans we desire development. That requires we evolve from struggle, into success, then significance, and ultimately, leaving a legacy. In this profession there is *always* a higher level (the sky is the limit). Who else could you benefit if you raised your level of success?

- You think you have done all that you are capable of doing - there are no barriers to your improvement. Think back to a time where you had to "dig deep" and did...and success followed. Burnout is a symptom of wasted energy and ineffective effort. You are only *one evolved* thought from demonstrating a higher level of effectiveness and success. You have to be committed to finding the "right way" and engage it through effort.

o *Mental conditioning* (Yellow Light) - there are many who are hungry for success and are willing to work to achieve it. The combination of energy and ethics are powerful raw materials that can help you double your revenue. Energy ensures you will work hard and ethics makes sure you don't cut corners. Since this challenge is mental, let's review the core "rationales";

▪ Pavlov Ian conditional reflex - You know the one - "ring the bell - feed the dog". Ring the bell...$50k...Ring the bell...$50k. After weeks, months, or years of a certain experience (income), we begin to believe this is all we are capable of producing. The mind begins to self-fulfill the outcome ($50k) and our effort increases but our effectiveness goes down...all in an effort to keep us where we are....ring the bell...$50k. You can re-condition your mind and develop new approaches that can break you out of stasis and propel you to higher achievement.

▪ Self-Image - the by-product of conditioning and sets the thermostat for what you can achieve in any area of your life. Can't see yourself losing that last 10 pounds...having a great relationship with your son...or generating a 6 or 7 figure income? *Guess what?* It won't happen until you see it in your mind...*first!* What you are capable of and what you believe you deserve is governed by your mind. As it relates to revenue (income), do you have Commaitis (a fear of commas)?

• Write down a "$1". Add zeros and commas (when necessary) to make a proper financial number. *When do you become uncomfortable?* $1,000 (a week) ... $10,000 (a month) ... $100,000 (a year) ... $10,000,000 (net worth in 10 years)... you get the picture! Begin to see bigger numbers of possibility in your life!

▪ <u>Fear</u> - the side-effect of Pavlov Ian conditioning and a shrinking self-image. We get stuck in paralysis by analysis, make a series of excuses for inaction and we become victims of circumstance. Introspection will reveal that fear is about a lack of and effective strategy and process to follow. Through evaluation you determined areas where you were excellence and areas of challenge. Two ways to achieve more - become exceptional at what you do best and/or get better (or get help) with the things that are not core strengths. Fear cannot be the excuse!!!

○ **Focus** (Green Light) - the key to evolving in your business is to get clear on what you want, why it is important and determining what is in your current environment that can help you get it. Once established, you must begin taking tangible action today! **<u>Nothing can stop you if it can be done and someone else is doing it!</u>** Don't focus on the industry or the economy - there are successful people in every upturn and downturn (sometimes more so in "corrections"). Don't focus on your neighbor - they are wrestling with their own issues! Don't focus on what you can't do - focus on possibilities and opportunities and develop a Can Do/Must Do attitude...*Evolve!*

This concludes Day Two

"How am I going to double myincome when I haven't even been in the business a year? I know I walked in here declaring that I would be a 7-figure producer, but now that I am *living it*, I realize how that must have sounded," Brad said contritely.

"While we could chalk that up to the exuberance of youth, *you had the right idea to think big*," responded Suzy. "Admittedly, I have only allowed myself to think of minimal success...to be average."

"Funny thing, the internal posting got my attention by listing the average salary of the first year sales person," chimed in David. "It was so much higher than my salary in operations that I salivated at the prospect of being even *less than average.* I think that has ruled my self-image and efforts to this point."

"*Does anyone of us just want to be average?*" Matt interjected. "I sure don't. We are working too hard to just be middle of the pack. No offense to the other recruits, or even those that have been here a while, but I want this bad and I am willing to do what it takes to be successful."

"Evolving is about determining what defines that success from a revenue perspective and then we will build strategies that back into that number. If we know the average revenue for a first year associate, then why don't we just double that number?" said Brad. "That average salary means some people are lower than that number -"

"And some are higher!" exclaimed David. "I want to be higher...that would change my life exponentially for the better."

"Ok, we all have our targets. Tomorrow we get into the Expand section where I think we will find answers on how we will all do this!"

E⁴ Boot Camp - Day #3

It was Thursday morning and the group was gathering for another day of the E⁴ boot camp. Matt was preparing the documents for the meeting, David was setting up the coffee, and Suzy was preparing the whiteboard for another round of brainstorming. Just then, Brad walked in with a deli tray with sandwiches and salad for lunch.

"Sorry I am a few minutes late, but I wanted to provide food today in anticipation that we will need to work through lunch today."

"It's only 7:25, but isn't it strange that you would now think 5 minutes early *is late* - my, how good habits form quickly," complimented Suzy.

"Yes, I think we are all picking up some good habits...he even brought salad for my benefit!" Matt said rubbing his stomach now 10 pounds lighter since he remained disciplined to his workouts and better eating regimens.

"Good morning everyone, " said Larry just turning the corner. "I see that the brood is still coming in early...commendable. Matt, have you heard from Mrs. Evans yet?"

"Not yet, I was hoping to hear from her by the end of the week."

"Send her a 'great meeting you card' to stimulate her action," Larry suggested.

"I did *that* yesterday! I actually found a card that had a series of smiling faces that said 'Make someone happy today' to remind her of my Happy People Program," Matt said proudly.

"Well, I'll be...I may actually have a professional partner for this one," Larry said with a pleased smile on his face.

As Larry walked out of the room, the other three gave Matt a high five and quietly applauded his victory. Now it was time for another day of planning. Brad goes to the front of the room to read;

Day #3 Expand - *Expansion is about progressively more highly effective activity for your business.* It is about growing revenue by increasing resources to areas that generate revenue and lowering efforts in those things that limit revenue. To grow your business you have to increase products, number of prospects (lead generation), close rate, persistency, and consistency of successful activity. Simultaneously, you have to decrease lost opportunity (such as cancellations), excuses and procrastination.

o **Increase your product offerings** - The quickest way to raise your revenue is to offer **more solutions** to *each client* you secure. If you have 300 clients and your single product commission is $250 then your annual income would be $75,000. Increase that to two products and it would only take 150 clients to earn the same $75,000...or you could still sell 300 and now earn $150,000! Studies of sales have proven that multiple sales to a single client has several benefits beyond higher revenue;

▪ Solidifies the relationship with the client resulting in higher persistency and fewer cancellations.

▪ Lower overall cost of acquisition and retention since cost of retaining clients is 1/5 the cost of obtaining a new one.

▪ Establishes you as a true professional and with ongoing communication, a Trusted Advisor.

▪ More fluid sales cycle with resulting referrals – which means higher close rates with less effort and cost.

○ **Take portfolio approach to products** - it is not enough (or ethical) to simply "pile on" products that do not have ultimate value to your client. You have to do the homework to understand your products intimately so that you can integrate them into the right solutions for your clients. You also have to dismiss your own internal price objections that you are "selling them too much". In most cases, you may actually save the client money by consolidating products, eliminating redundancy, and giving them one point of contact - you...as Trusted Advisor.

▪ Research your products and get someone versed in them to outline the ways it can be applied to various situations.

▪ Review competitive products and uncover ways that your products can meet your client's needs more comprehensively by consolidating products they own.

■ Conduct annual reviews for all your clients to determine if their needs have expanded.

o **Increase your prospects** (lead generation) - Depending on where you are in the sales development continuum there will be a preferred order of where your leads come from;

■ <u>Effort Phase</u> (Progressing through Order Taker to Lead Junkie Phases) - 1ˢᵗ 90 days – *When you are just starting out, you have to focus on lead opportunities that are plentiful and low cost.* If you are on straight commission, then you also need to focus on leads that are the **fast to obtain**. <u>The goal is to have as many experiences in as short a time frame as possible while progressively improving sales effectiveness (close rate)</u>. In the beginning, there should be a hierarchy of leads;

● **Telemarketing** (In-source) - This is the lowest cost, most plentiful, and "fastest to table" lead source. Yes, potentially the close rate will be low but it gives you a running start to build momentum.

● **Telemarketing appointment setting** (Out-source) - depending on your industry and the nature of your product there is likely a company that you can contract with to secure appointments. *This is not to be used to replace your own efforts, but to support them* - giving you more experiences and more closes (quickly). Due to cost and potential quality issues this source should not be relied on beyond the "gaining momentum" period.

- **Direct response** - Direct mail (and email) is a standard method to secure client opportunities on an ongoing basis. The drawbacks are a longer timeline for execution (creative development, mail time, and response), cost, and unpredictability of response rates. Like telemarketing, direct response is "science and art". Other forms are print, radio, television, and "click-through" internet advertising.

- **Networking** - This is more than just handing out business cards at the Rotary Club. It should be a synergistic, mutually beneficial series of relationships that bring you before broader audiences. Become the "go to" expert in circles of influence and be active in your community. This should be done in proper proportion as many sales people *only network* and don't engage the other prospecting methods. As a guideline (or rule!), 75% of your time should be "one on one" engagements, 15% for networking, and 10% chasing "The Big One".

- **Repeat business** - to "help fewer clients with more" is the most efficient way to progress from Order Taker to Trusted Advisor. The clients you obtain through the various sources should be your first line opportunities for additional product placements.

- **Referrals** - Ask any sales professional and they will tell you that referrals are the *lowest cost/highest close rate* opportunities. Yes, to get referrals you have to have a base of clients. Yet, many do not cultivate the relationships necessary to secure referrals...*many never even ask for them!* **Don't let that be you...ask for referrals!!!**

■ <u>Skill Phase</u> (Progressing to Professional to Trusted Advisor) - As you progress in skill your lead sources should work *inversely* from that of someone new in the business and in the effort phase. You still have to work <u>all</u> lead sources (I know high producers that still prospect!) to ensure a growing business. *However, your primary sources should be repeat business and referrals.* You invest a percentage (8-10%) of your revenue in the other sources.

o <u>Increase Persistency</u> - that "bird in the hand is worth five in the bush"! *Recent studies have shown that the cost of getting a new client is 5 times more costly than keeping current ones.* The key to maintaining your client base (from which to generate referrals!) is;

■ Follow-up and conduct ongoing communications
■ Sell them other products (Trusted Advisor)

o <u>Increase your close rate</u> - the single greatest way to increase sales is to increase *your effectiveness*...**your close rate**. The other elements we have examined will help you get to the root cause of the "science of selling" but it is harder to get to the bottom of any issues that may exist with your artful "sales voice". It is also easy for sales people to blame a lost sale on their potential clients - "*they didn't buy*" is the common refrain. Many are oblivious to the real issue - "*I didn't sell*". Through the process of evaluation (Day #1) you should have uncovered some potential causes for a low close rate by lead channel and product. They will fall into two broad categories;

➤**Gap in product knowledge** - it will be hard to sound compelling or convincing if you don't know your product and its benefits to your potential clients. This is easy to remedy...*study your products!!! Know your products!!! Buy your products and experience them for yourself!*

▪ **Not asking for the sale** - there comes a point in every interaction where you have to conclude by <u>asking</u> for their business. Relaxing, Relating and even Releasing your solution is pointless if you don't *ask*. Though there are countless ways to close and every sales person has their own "best close" recipe, there are only two ways to Get Better at closing - practice and direct experience.

• Practice should involve role playing with your manager or colleagues. You should have a list of the top 10 objections (*there are only so many*) and then come up with persuasive points of view to demonstrate overriding value. Ask the top agents (over lunch - you pay!) how they would answer the objections. Then practice, practice, practice...until they are 1ˢᵗ nature and in your "own voice".

• Experience truly is the best teacher but you have to be careful not to ingrain bad habits and squander too many opportunities. You can request a manager go with you on key sales opportunities, or split commission with a more seasoned veteran and let them monitor and "save" your sale.

o Increase your consistency - Some sales people, even the very successful ones are in a form of stasis - *they are not developing or improving.* Physical workouts are most beneficial in a cumulative manner, if they are consistent. The best performers in any craft are constantly improving themselves. Every day do something to Get Better in key areas - but increased knowledge is crucial. The key to skill development is to improve your inherent understanding of your product, industry, competition and the sales process (effectiveness).

This concludes Day 3

"That was eye opening!" said Matt. "Particularly in the area of lead generation...I have only used my own telemarketing up to now."

"It's great to think that we can outsource some of this or use mediums like direct mail - but that costs money," said David. "Suzy, you have the most sales of the group, what do you think?"

"Ironically, I had ust reached out to the marketing department for an explanation of the direct mail lead program that we can tap into. She seemed surprised to get the call since only the proven producers seem to use it. I agree with David that cost was a primary consideration and I was waiting on a few more sales before I invested in it," she relayed.

"How does it work?" asked Brad.

"They will send out a minimum of 10,000 well crafted, direct mail pieces to your pre-determined zip codes and product preferences. They will space them out over a 4 week period. It is very targeted and specific," she added.

"*What is the response rate?*" Matt asked.

"Whoa! Somebody paid attention during the science of direct mail portion of the program!" laughed David.

"It depends on the list criteria and other factors, but she told me the average was 2%. She then said the close rate was very good at 60% - that was based on top producers close rates. Since I am still developing, I would think my close rate would be lower...about 40%"

"That would still be 200 opportunities with 80 closes!" exclaimed Brad punching the calculator on his Smartphone. "Ok, now the BIG question...*the cost?*"

"Well, that was my sticking point," Suzy began. "The company will pay for everything *except postage*. They will get presorted rates so it would be $2,500 for the 10,000 minimum pieces. Oh yes, they will take it from the base salary...after taxes of course. One more kicker - she has 16 pre-set appointments for this Monday that she is desperate for someone to run, but we would have to be a part of the lead program. I can let her know today. Yes, my mathematicians, that would be 4 leads each."

They all looked at each other with a glance representative of this critical moment of truth...

"$625 each...*a mere pittance*," Matt invited their response by putting his hand out for them to pile on like a baseball team before the World Series game 7.

One by one, they added their hands to his and with a shout and a throwing up of their hands - they had just raised the stakes...*and their opportunity for success!*

E⁴ Boot Camp - Day #4

Happy Friday everyone, Matt said enthusiastically greeting the assembling group. "Happy Friday!" they chorused. "I don't know about all of you, but I feel change is in the air," added Matt. "Today we get ready for an explosion!"

"Well, I thought there would be an explosion last night when I told my wife that my check would be debited $625 a month for leads," chuckled David. "Her real reaction was one of support and that she believed this was the start I needed to breakout. Funny, *I believe it now, too!* Today is my day to lead so let's get started!"

Explode - The first three days were focused on determining where you are today (Evaluate), where you want to go (Evolve) and how to get there (Expand). Today we will "split the atom" of your business and help it Explode! The best way to explode your business is to do one simple thing...*treat it like a business!* Sounds elementary, but <u>many sales people are production minded and not business minded</u>. Even if you work for a company, you are the "wheel within a wheel" and responsible for your business growth and development. Robert Kiyosaki in Rich Dad, Poor Dad instructs us to create business systems and not just "own a job". Great advice. Business Mastery is the uranium that will generate great force in your business with a focus on core concepts;

o **Law of Multiplied Effort** - businesses of all sizes endeavor to increase revenue. The local "five and dime" has visions of grandeur as the next Wal-Mart or IKEA. They want to scale their business (grow) and use economies of scale to "*be everywhere*". Effort has to be efficient and once the secret sauce is ready...that effort must be multiplied to go from local, to regional, to national. On a smaller scale (unless you dream of being the national or international) you can do this with your business by becoming more *efficient and effective*. The following are a series of ideas that can be implemented at various stages of your business development;

Time management - Use of the precious commodity of time determines levels of success. You are the revenue generator for your business and your time is best spent *generating revenue*. Time maximization techniques;

▪ If you are engaged in telemarketing or a series of calls, then you need a more efficient process to generate better results. Invest in a good phone headset and leave it on during concentrated call times – focus . The better ones snap off for the necessary bathroom breaks but stay on your head in "ready mode".

▪ Looking for numbers and dialing rob you of precious time. Utilize CRM (Client Relationship Management) software to load all your calls for instant, successive dialing efforts. Most of these programs also have a drop down menu to schedule appointments and call disposition for tracking (Evaluating) your results.

■ Internet based call routing systems can improve your image and allow you to only take the most important calls. Yes, phone menus can be a put off, but you can always start by saying "press # to get to me directly". Many of your calls are people who may only want to leave messages anyway.

■ Voicemail to Email can be the answer for busy sales professionals who receive a bevy of voicemails each day. Cueing them up, writing down notes are all tedious and time consuming. There are programs that will convert voicemail to emails where they can be managed more efficiently in your inbox.

■ Email management - A class on Outlook will pay dividends for the busy sales professional. Setting up rules to route emails into categories, preview options, and other valuable tools allow you to read what matters most....*quickest*. Many people have multiple accounts that can be consolidated to arrive in <u>one</u> main account. There should also be preset times of the day to read and answer emails that don't adversely impact your day. When your assistant (yes you need one!) is proficient, they can even review and answer them for you!

■ Use <u>one</u> calendar system. Outlook is the leading program, and can be synced in a myriad of ways - even to phones and tablets. You can give sharing permissions so your assistant, or others can have access (you determine how much!) to your schedule.

▪ Make use of The Cloud. If you travel and don't always have access to your full computer (think phone or tablet), you can transfer your most important documents to Cloud technology. Your files and even functional versions of popular software can be accessed remotely. If you have an assistant, you can share documents easily and collaborate, seamlessly. The benefits are vast and it also creates a safe backup haven for all of your critical documents.

Outsource - the key question to ask before outsourcing is "can someone else do this?" If the answer is yes, then you can recover more time to generate revenue.

➤Hire an assistant. The average sales person's day is filled with a plethora of non-revenue generating activities. Paperwork (even if by computer) can be arduous as many sales people are "two finger typists" and can't find the backspace button! Even entering a sale (a joyous event!) can rob you of the time to make 100 prospecting calls, 2 demonstrations and one group seminar. <u>Hire an assistant to do all of the things that pull you from your highest and best use</u>. *Can't afford it?* Group share an assistant. If your business model will allow you can contract a virtual assistant on an "as needed" basis. *Regardless, an assistant will easily pay for itself over time!*

▪ Contract with a lead development and/or marketing company. The key to keeping your opportunity pipeline filled is to be consistent and effective with marketing and lead generation. It can also help you establish a polished image and brand. They can help you develop a consistent prospecting system, create (and monitor results) a good direct mail program, and provide a turnkey referral program.

■ Crowd source for great ideas and professional polish. Google "crowd sourcing" and you will see a flourishing world of contractors who are ready to convert your rough ideas into finished brochures, print media, and even videos! For most of these sites, you post your project and what you are willing to pay and in a few days your inbox is filled with detailed proposals - amazing!

Utilize technology - Technology should be engaged to make your business *efficient*. The internet is the platform that makes it scalable...worldwide. There are a few basic tools every business needs;

■ Website - simple or complex, this "destination" can tell your story, establish your expertise, and even take orders! More importantly, they can help you build your database of potential clients.

■ Social Media - a logical extension of your website are the exponentially expansive fixtures of social media to include Facebook, Twitter, YouTube and a wave of others. Thankfully, you can outsource the design of websites and these perquisite social media platforms.

- CRM (Client Relationship Management) technology can help you build your database of clients, stay in contact with them via email, and create unique interactions with individuals or groups.

- Webinar and online video call technology is fantastic to create professional meetings and streaming content to educate, inform, and sell your potential clients. The ease of use of these tools should remove any technology fears and they allow you to "see" more people and tell your unique story!

- Blogs can help establish you as an expert and give clients and potential clients a reason to visit you often to read your pearls o' wisdom. You can also tap the content of professional bloggers and add that to your online presence.

Personal Development - Ultimately, *you* are the product that people buy. You have to invest in yourself just as you would in direct marketing. Your goal is to build your brand and position yourself as an expert in the eyes of your client, your community, and your industry. You can invest in self-development programs, hire a coach, and attend conventions and workshops. **You must continue to improve and the resulting changes will fuel your business' success to the next level – to help it Explode!**

Congratulations! This concludes Day Four and the E4 Program

As David finished reading the material, there was a collective sigh of relief, exhaustion and satisfaction. Matt broke the silence, "I don't know about you guys, but this has been an eye-opening experience!"

"Yes, and a wallet opening one...almost everything we need to do to grow our business will take money," replied Brad.

"I am certain your rich father would tell you it takes money to make money," laughed Suzy playfully, "*All businesses have to put in before they can take out.*"

"Yes, but we can't do an IPO to raise money like they do!" replied David. "However, there are things here that I know make sense as they help operationalize the sales process and could make our lives easier as we focus on sales."

"I agree that many of these things sound out of reach from a cost perspective, but the successful people in the office are doing it," began Matt. "Like Jack Jeffries said 'we won't all be Larry Wilcox, but we *can be*.' He invests in his success, and to model his behavior, we have to do the same things. *If you are not prepared to invest in your success, you will never achieve any.*"

"A lesson from LeRoy no doubt," said Brad. "I want to be like Larry one day, too, but he has the advantage of the company paying for all his perks...*like his assistant.*"

"Ahem!" said Larry's assistant who had just walked up to the door of the conference room. "Actually, Larry hired me after he was here *only* 3 weeks. He brought me on in a part-time basis and paid me on his own dime. Once he became more successful, he engaged me full-time – still on his dime, and shortly thereafter told the company to hire me directly. From the beginning, he told me my job was to free him up to do what he does *best* - building relationships, solving problems and meeting needs. Speaking of needs, Matt you have a guest at the receptionist desk."

"See, I have an assistant already!" exclaimed Matt who hurried to the front to find Mrs. Evans sitting in a chair reading a magazine.

"Mrs. Evans...Happy Friday and great to see you!" said Matt shocked that she had come to the office herself.

"There you go with that 'Happy' business. I had a meeting at the office building next door and decided to pop in."

"Would you like something to drink?"

"No, I have to run, but wanted to set the stage for my review of your services as a Generational Wealth Specialist. I will be travelling for the next week but wanted to give you the card of my COO, Myrtle Hicks, who will review everything and pull me in for the ultimate decision meeting. She is expecting your call on Monday at 9:30am to set an appointment to begin the proceedings."

"Wonderful, I look forward to speaking with her and presenting what we can do for your company. Have a great weekend and a safe and productive trip!"

"Is he always this enthusiastic?" inquired Mrs. Evans to the receptionist. With an affirmative nod confirming her assumption, she shook Matt's hand and left for her trip.

Act II - A Day in the Life!

Get your house in order

Matt arrived at the office at 7:30am according to his new schedule. Today proved the effectiveness of getting an early start as he had 4 appointments to run on his desk from the lead program and lots of other things to accomplish. A quick review of his list on his Smartphone;

- 7:30am - Prepare for meetings with Daniel and the team at the barbershop and Mr. Jacob's Rotary Club

- 9:00am - Sales meeting

- 9:30am - Call Myrtle Hicks at the Evans Agency to set up initial meeting

- 12:00 - Lunch (Turkey on whole wheat, apple, water)

Today's Appointments

- 10:30am - James Francis, son of Beverly and Steve Francis to review transfer of retirement accounts

- 1:00pm - Heather and Zach Thomas - recently married looking for life insurance

- 3:00pm - David Branch - questions about his deceased father's account - wanted someone to come out to explain.

- 4:30pm - Doris Clemmons - shopping several carriers and wants full needs analysis

The sales meeting went as usual with recognition of all the upcoming activity that Matt reported. Seeing it reflected on the board and on his schedule gave him a sense of how activity *should* correspond to results. There was so much to do that he didn't even have time to review his appointments. He wouldn't get to do call planning, which he knew was important, but he also didn't have time to prejudge the leads either. Many of the newer agents would stare at the leads trying to determine buyer receptivity from a lifeless piece of paper. He would simply get there at the appointed time...ready to service the client's needs. It was 9:30am and time to call Ms. Hicks. He thought he should be nervous as the number rang through, but he wasn't. He and Mrs. Evans had hit it off so well and he felt there would be a carryover effect with the other people in her office...starting with Ms. Hicks.

"Good morning, you have reached the Evans Agency...this is Maggie, how may I direct your call?"

"Happy Monday Maggie, this is Matthew Palmer and I have a 9:30 call with Myrtle Hicks."

"Yes, Mr. Palmer, she is expecting you. I will put you right through."

"Thank you!" said Matt marveling at the professionalism and image the agency exhibited...*just from a simple phone call.*

"Mr. Palmer, this is Myrtle Hicks," she said in a very stoic *business only* tone.

"Happy Monday Ms. Hicks and please call me Matt. I understand from Mrs. Evans that you are the company's COO and will be helping me facilitate a proposal for the Evans Agency."

"That is correct," she answered dryly, "She is travelling this week but wants to wrap this up by next Friday and then make a decision. Be clear, we have been with our current broker 15 years I am quite satisfied. Mrs. Evans is allowing this proposal based on her brief interaction with you. That said - *what will you need from us?*"

Matt was thrown off by the cold delivery but realized that as the gatekeeper to the company, she was probably inundated with offers, solicitations and every conceivable pitch.

"I will need detailed demographic information on the agency, its employees and independent agents. I would also need a copy of the employee handbook and other information that will outline the current programs. Who will be my primary contact for this information and anything else I need?" Matt asked transitioning to a business tone to match hers.

"You can get in touch with Leanne Simpson who handles all of our Human Resources needs. I will let her know you will be in touch with her for this information. When should I tell her to expect you?"

"Alert her to Thursday at 1pm."

"Mr. Palmer, is there anything else you will need from me?"

"No Ms. Hicks...I think that will give me everything I will need -"

"Then we will see you next Friday at 10am for you to deliver the proposal, "she hung up before he could utter thank you.

Larry had just walked over knowing that Matt had the initial call. "Ms. Hicks is a monster of a gatekeeper isn't she?" Larry said knowingly from direct experience.

"More like a Barbarian at the Gate!" Matt said breathing a sigh of relief that the call was over. "We have an appointment set up for next Friday at 10am to deliver a proposal."

"Whoa, that would be record time for preparing a proposal for an opportunity that big. Besides, Fridays are my personal recovery days...*remember?* Since this is an account that has eluded me for 5 years and you have gotten this far, I will make an exception."

"That is reassuring," Matt said relieved. "This is all so new and while I am not afraid to take the necessary steps, I don't know all the things to consider. I have to meet with the H.R person, Leanne Simpson, on Thursday at 1pm. I tried to buy some time before that meeting to get some things together."

"*Can I give you a word of advice?*" Larry uncharacteristically asking for permission to proceed.

"As many words as you are willing to give...I am all ears!" Matt answered hungrily.

"To pull this account off you need to be polished, organized and highly effective. Right now, I see you extremely *busy* but not as *effective* as you should be. The single best thing you could do right now is multiply yourself with a skilled assistant."

"Strange you should mention that...we just reviewed a program that said the same thing. I understand that you hired your assistant about the same time as where I am right now. I can see the value, but I am not sure how I can afford it."

"*If a man is not willing to invest in his success, he will never have any*," answered Larry without one trace of sympathy. "I will do you one better, here is the number for Anna Jones who was an assistant to the top rep in California. She moved here a year ago and just had a baby and needs flexible hours...she would be perfect for you," Larry said confidently.

"*How will I pay her?*" Matt asked seeing money going out but not coming in.

"You will pay her with money, dinero...moola," he answered snidely. "Look Matt, as a business owner you have to be prepared to invest in your business. You will figure it out, but make the call. My work here is done. Oh yes, see you at 7:30am tomorrow so we can map out the Evans Agency proposal."

"I have a presentation tomorrow at 9:00am, can we make it Wednesday?"

"You obviously didn't put that on the shared Outlook calendar because you looked open...*you really need an assistant.* Ok, Wednesday it is - that is my last concession!" he said firmly. Matt knew his patience was wearing thin.

Matt was starting to spin from the frenetic pace of all that was going on. Remembering how he had forgotten the Miller's Family Parents Night Out a few weeks ago with Erin, he knew that his mind was sharp - *just filled with too much information.* He couldn't afford to slip on anything else. He marveled at how Larry always seemed to be under control and efficient. He knew it was time to go to the next level, so he looked at the number he had just received and dialed the number to call Anna.

"Good morning and Happy Monday Anna, this is Matt Palmer -"

"Happy Monday to you Matt! Larry said that you would call," answered Anny with a voice of enthusiasm.

"Is this a good time for you?" Matt could hear a baby crying in the background.

"Sorry about that, the baby is just teething and a little cranky but this is fine. *I hear you desperately need an assistant and I desperately need a job.* To give you my background, I have 5 years experience with the company, in-depth knowledge of the products, policies and procedures. I worked with the top rep in

California, so I have also vicariously learned the best sales tactics. I will become an extension of you and your business - representing you professionally with each interaction. I also know that you are just getting started and in my current situation with little Jonathon, I need flexibility but envision myself growing with you. I have heard great things about you from Larry and he says you are an up and comer."

"All of that sounds great and I can tell just from this interaction and Larry's high regard of you that you would be perfect," Matt's was thrilled about the possibility of having someone so polished on his team. It would be a great advantage.

"Great! All that we need to figure out is when you want me to start and my pay," Anna said matter of fact assuming they had closed the deal.

"As for start date, Wednesday morning would be perfect as I have a major account I am preparing for -"

"*The Evans account?* I have spoken to Larry's assistant and I think we can do a great job readying the proposal."

"Wow, you're really on it! Regarding pay...here's the thing -"

"Look Matt, as you can see, *we both need this relationship.* I would be willing to come in and show what I can do for you for 1 week. If you don't see my value and how I will pay for myself 10 times over we can end it...no questions asked."

"Wow, you are good...how could I possibly say no to that offer," he said realizing she was willing to put her skill to the test.

"The classic Demonstration Close - once they try it out they will buy it! Just one of the lessons learned watching the best sales people in action. See you Wednesday at 8:00am and I am looking forward to working with you!"

"Yes...me too Anna!" Matt realized that opportunities like this don't come around often and that is was time for him to step up his game and get his house in order.

A house divided...

Matt reached the home of Beverly and Steve Francis at 10:20am and rang the doorbell. "Good morning, my name is Matthew Palmer, here for a 10:30 appointment."

"Perfect timing, young man," said Mrs. Francis. "Our son isn't here yet but come on in. Steve is out back in the garden doing his daily weeding."

"Well, I have to tell you the yard is beautiful," Matt complimented. "My mom would have a fit over the roses that cover the carriage house...*they are spectacular!*"

"Those roses are the pride of my garden," said Mr. Francis entering the kitchen where Matt had laid his briefcase on the breakfast table. "New Dawn and -"

"Lady Banks...*right?*" interjected Matt like he was on a game show.

"A man that knows his roses...are you into gardening?" asked Mr. Francis.

"Only when my mother makes me! You guys work too hard for me!" Matt answered laughing.

"A good son!" added Mrs. Francis. "Speaking of sons, ours will be here in a few minutes. He insists on being involved as we contemplate making some changes to our financial picture. We have been retired for 4 years and lost quite a bit of money in all of the financial calamity."

"Yes, he insists on being here. Not sure if he is trying to protect us, or preserve our money to make sure we leave more to him," says Mr. Francis with a huff.

"Don't air our dirty laundry in front of Matt," whispered Mrs. Francis to her husband pulling playfully on his shirt.

Just then their son, James Francis, walked in and blurted out, "I hope you guys have not started without me, and for God's sake haven't signed anything!"

"We were waiting on you and just talking about their beautiful roses. Mr. Francis, my name is Matthew Palmer," he said extending his hand that was left un-shaken.

"Roses, huh? Step one, build rapport, step two...fleece two elderly people, right? I've been in sales and I know how this works. Your business card says you are a Generational Wealth Specialist - what does that mean *exactly*."

Matt resisted the urge to meet his cynicism with defense or offense. Instead he did what he knew to do...he used his authentic voice;

"As a Generational Wealth Specialist, my primary role will be helping your parents provide for their current lifestyle needs, protect their hard-earned wealth from additional risk, and preserve it to be passed on to future generations. I understand your suspicions about the current state of affairs.

There were decades when people like your parents did all the right things, following what appeared to be sound advice...and then the game changed dramatically. That is regretful, but saying sorry to someone that has lost wealth is a small consolation. *What needs to happen now?* A thorough review of your parent's resources, their risk tolerances and needs/goals should be blended into a comprehensive plan that can be implemented and, more importantly, understood by all involved."

"That is what we want, too," said the elder Mr. Francis. "I like the way you answered that. It would do our minds good to actually understand what we invest in this time. *What would it take for you to do a full review?*"

"Not so fast, dad," interjected his son, "I don't want all your information floating around with too many of these brokers. Matt, no offense, but you look all of 25 and probably inexperienced. My parents have sizeable assets and we need to be sure we get with someone who knows what they are doing."

Matt was reminded of LeRoy's lessons about Relaxing and disconnecting from the outcome of the sales. *The worst thing that could happen is that he walked out with some rose clippings to give his mother.* At this moment, his Desired Outcome was simply to get a Needs Analysis started...*not actually sell them anything.*

"Let me give a little information on myself, the company, and the process we would use. I have a degree in Finance from Fulbright College, our company is highly rated, even in this economic environment, and all cases the size of your parents go through three levels of review before final submission and approval. In fact, you will have access to some of the best financial minds in the world. We would also evaluate your situation no less than annually with a personal review to make sure your goals are being met or make adjustments.

Candidly, Mr. Francis, I don't think yours is an issue of my experience, *but one of trust.* Trust is something built on integrity and sincerity...not solely experience. *You should run from anyone that promises your parents won't lose money.* No one is in that position. My promise to you is to leverage my company's vast resources and products to develop a strong plan. More importantly, I will take the time needed to explain it to you and your parent's satisfaction. If that sounds like an approach that warrants additional discovery, then I would be honored to assist. The analysis does not obligate you in any way, but will reveal strategies that can accomplish your goals. *Based on that, it is entirely up to you if we should continue?*" Matt concluded with silence waiting for them to answer.

After moments of awkward glances between them, Mrs. Francis spoke directly to her husband. "My vote is yes - I like the way he sounds and eventually we will have to trust someone, *right Steve?*"

"Yes Beverly, I agree," he began. "James, we have both done extensive research on Matt's company and in these few minutes, I feel like he is a young man we can work with - or at least figure out if it makes sense to do business with him. What happened last time was unfortunate, *but we've gotten over it*. In retrospect, the losses were partly the result of us not continuing to review our program on an annual basis. I like the fact that Matt will come out to see us and he is young enough to be around," he said with a wink in Matt's direction.

"You two are pushovers. Matt will only focus on products that generate the most commission and not in your best interest," James said angrily now that the two of them had voted him down.

"It is true, that I derive part of my living from the programs we will develop and implement," Matt answered. "Those choices will only be governed by your goals with provision, protection and preservation as the *key determining factors*. Mr. Francis, it is much like your garden of roses. You plant them, feed them and weed them to give them the right environment for growth. You also have to do annual pruning and cut back the areas that don't perform as they should - robbing other more fruitful branches of precious growing power. Your reward for that dedication of time and energy is -"

"A flourishing garden," finished Mr. Francis nodding his head affirmatively.

"It will be no different for me and my compensation. *If I serve...I deserve*. I know there is a lot at stake for the decisions you have to make. Let me give you all a few minutes alone to discuss next steps." Matt headed out the kitchen door to have a walk in the garden. He noticed the beauty of the day and the awesome spectacle of the Francis' garden. He also chuckled to himself that he had really stopped to smell the roses. Amazingly, he really wasn't stressed over the last few minutes and the possible outcome - he had relaxed, related, and released to the best of his ability. *Now it was up the client.*

"Young man, we *all* think it prudent that we proceed with you," said the elder Mr. Francis walking out on the patio. "I think we all have a level of comfort with you as our trusted advisor."

"Wonderful! I will take some initial information for the financial review, and once completed, we can walk through the recommendations. My assistant Anna will schedule a follow-up time for all of us to evaluate my findings. Let's get started!"

Now...and later

Matt had finished his turkey sandwich and was brushing his teeth using a travel kit he had gotten from Tom, his brother in law, at Christmas. "A good sales person *never* has bad breath," Tom said. Sure came in handy now that he was a road warrior. He pulled up to the home of Heather and Zach Thomas who had just gotten married and needed life insurance. The lead didn't say much else, so Matt picked up his briefcase and headed up the walkway to their side of a duplex.

He noticed a ninja-style motorcycle on the porch next to the door. As he admired it, a voice came out from behind the screen door, "A beauty isn't she?"

"Power and precision in a stunning package...*what is not to like?* My name is Matt and I am here for our 1:00pm appointment. You must be the fast and furious Zach Thomas?" Matt reached past the door to shake his hand and Zach shook it warmly.

"That would be me. This is my wife Heather. *Do you ride?*"

"I have always wanted to, but alas, it was only a romantic notion. Truth be told, my wife shut it down quickly as too dangerous *for me.*"

"See Zach, it's not just me that thinks it is too dangerous!" blurted his wife.

"I have been riding since I was 6 years old, I grew up around them. I agree that someone just getting started should not be getting a fast bike like this one, but in the hands of an expert, it is safe," Zach defending his ability and his sport.

"I don't mind him riding, but I want him to get insurance to protect me and our future family in case something does happen. My father has insurance with your company so I called last week to get you out here today - *we need insurance!*" Heather said emphatically.

"And I say we can't afford it right now. I agree with you that I should get covered...eventually. As newly married folks, we have to prioritize where our money goes. I just can't see paying money for something that *might happen* versus paying for the things that *are happening*. You know I love you and want to take care of you. Nothing will happen to me on this bike...promise," Zach said taking her hand and kissing her forehead.

"I understand everything you both have said," began Matt. "Heather your concern about Zach and the future reminds me of my wife, Erin. She can see the bills coming 3 months out, while I focus on today. Zach, I agree your riding expertise makes you less likely to have an accident, but we cover more than just things that might happen on the bike. *Life is funny and unpredictable.* One minute you are healthy and enjoying life and then the unexpected happens. I don't believe in scaring people to buy insurance, but I do remind them that life can change...*quickly*. You also remind me of myself - a man determined to provide for your family...now and later. Together you make a great team," said Matt sincerely.

"You hit the nail on the head, but the real question is still *how we can afford it?*" asked Zach scratching his head.

"Since we are past of the point of *what we need* and *why we need it*, the only thing left is 'how' to pay," began Matt. "*Are you both employed right now?*"

"Yes. Zach has a good job as a mechanic at a big auto dealership in town and I am just getting started with nursing at the hospital," answered Heather. "The real problems are my student loans and the tools we had to buy for Zach. In another year, we will be in great shape, but working in the hospital, I see firsthand that things do change quickly as you said."

"Do your companies offer benefits?" Matt inquired probing for viable alternatives and the big picture.

"Yes, they do. I took the single coverage only option for healthcare and declined everything else - it was too expensive," Zach responded.

"My benefit options become live next month and I will be putting both of us on the hospitals healthcare plan. It is better than what he has at his job," said Heather.

"Great decision as healthcare is an important foundation of comprehensive coverage," reassured Matt. "There are other things that you will want to add over time besides healthcare. Life insurance is probably offered by both companies...*right?*"

"Yes, it was an option but I checked 'no'. It may not be too late to add it though. *Do you think I should add it?*" asked Heather looking for Matt to lead them in the right direction.

"Yes, I think you *both* should add it. Zach, now that Heather can cover you with healthcare you can save money by dropping your single coverage. Since you have had a qualifying life change of marriage, you should be able to make changes outside of the annual election period. Take the money you save from dropping that single health coverage and use that premium to buy the highest face value of term insurance possible. With your age and good health that should be $100,000 to $200,000 of coverage. Essentially budget neutral...*would that work?*"

"Are you kidding? That's perfect!" exclaimed Zach. "Look, I could turn your car on and tell you in 30 seconds of listening to the engine what might be wrong, but this financial stuff is out of my comfort zone."

"We all have our gifts and as we use them to help others they provide us a valuable way to make a living," Matt emphasized.

"Matt, that all makes great sense and brings me great peace," said Heather hugging his neck.

"Great, then my work here is done...*for now*. Call me if you have questions about the coverage they offer and I will do my best to answer or point you in the right direction. Also, if you don't mind, I will keep in touch with you over time to see if things change or if there are other ways I can help you. This covers you for *now*...we can focus on the ultimate future...*later*."

"Not to worry, call anytime and I will tell my friends about you and how helpful you have been," remarked Heather seeing him to the door.

"Yeah man, you are the kind of person I like doing business with so you are always welcome," said Zach shaking his hand.

As he walked down the sidewalk to his car, Matt felt a great satisfaction. Sure he didn't get the sale, but he gained much more - he helped two people that needed his knowledge. He knew that the genuine help he offered *now* would turn into a great client...*later*. He also realized that how he found a quick solution to resolve the challenges for the Thomas' would be the same process he would use to figure out how to afford Anna as his assistant. For now, it was time for the next appointment.

More than expected

The appointment with the Thomas' was over much sooner than he expected, so he decided to use the extra 30 minutes to figure out how he could afford Anna. He was already obligated to $625 a month for the lead program and that was going to be tough. Since the average commission opportunity was $400 and using the breakeven formula from his days at Fulbright, he realized that he would only need 2 sales to at least get back that investment. The team had projected 25 leads each so that would only be a closing rate of 10%! He laughed at the absurdity of how "easy" that should be. Using a Revenue Projection formula he assumed a close rate of 50% which would result in 12 sales from the program. He would earn $4,800 gross revenue and net $4,175 after the investment. *Not bad!*

He then factored in his own telemarketing and networking efforts and realized that should generate another $3,000. Added together, it would *almost* reach the "double your income" number from Day 2 of the E⁴ boot camp. *Was that really possible?* As he focused on the math and played with the numbers, the reality of that possibility overwhelmed him. Certainly, he could afford Anna with that level of revenue and because he could actually be more efficient, *he might actually exceed it.* The mathematical process he used didn't even factor in the bigger cases, like the Evans Agency or Mr. and Mrs.

Francis from earlier in the day. This must have been what Jack Jeffries meant when he said "opportunity is now here." *Matt now truly believed it, too!*

At 2:50pm Matt rang the doorbell for his appointment. "Good afternoon Mr. Branch, my name is Matthew Palmer here for your 3:00pm appointment."

"Thanks for being on time. I apologize but I am in a hurry. I have a few questions about my father's account with your company and I didn't want to discuss it over the phone," he opened.

"I am truly sorry to hear about your father," said Matt sympathetically. "I will be glad to answer any questions I can for you."

"He actually died a few years ago, but I just found this policy a few days ago. Can you tell me what it is and what it means?" he asked handing Matt a thick stack of papers in a folder.

Matt took a few minutes to review the documents that Mr. Branch had given him. "Do you mind if I make a phone call to get a few more details?"

"No problem, I will go get ready as I have to leave in 30 minutes."

Matt dialed David's cell phone number knowing that he was out of the office on his 4 appointments as well. "Hey David, I know you are on the road...how is it going?"

"*Can you say two for two?*" David answered jubilantly. "These leads are terrific! Now that I am finally getting into the home, my operations experience is coming in quite handy!"

"I am glad the *sales* David is doing so well, but I need the *operations* David for a few minutes," Matt said playfully. "I have a contract here that looks to be from the early 70's and I am sure we no longer sell this type of policy. What can I do to find out what it is and what it is worth?"

"Let me conference us in with Bret in operations. He worked for me for many years and actually got promoted into my old spot...hold on." David dialed the number and patched Matt into the call.

"This is Bret in operations," said the third voice on the call.

"Hey Bret, this is David and I have Matt Palmer, sales guy extraordinaire on the line."

"Hey Matt...*what's up?*" Bret inquired.

I am at the home of David Branch and his father, Ronald Branch died a few years ago and has this policy with us from the 70's. I need to know what it is and its value."

"Easy. Give me the account number. Look on page 15 and down in section D, you should find it there" Bret directed realizing that as a newbie Matt likely had no idea where to find it.

"There it is, right where you said," Matt amazed at his proficiency.

"Give me a minute. There it is. *You won't believe this!* Based on the program and how it was funded, it is quite substantial. The interest rates generated and locked in periods for this account reached their peak in the Jimmy Carter era. The $25,000 he put in as a lump in 1970 sum along with additional contributions is now worth $750,000! Sue and David Branch are listed as beneficiaries, so payout would be simple. All we would need it the death certificate. I just emailed you the form they would need to your phone."

"Wow! I owe you lunch for your help. David said you were good and now I can see that for myself," Matt said sincerely.

"It's good to know people in low places," joked David. "Bret is great and as long as we don't wear him out, he will take our calls.""

"You guys just keep the sales coming and I will talk to you anytime you need me. Talk to you later."

"David, can you be in the office at 7:30am on Wednesday? Matt asked. "I have a proposition for you."

"Sure thing, but for now, two down and two more to go! Over and out!" closed David.

Just then Mr. Branch walked into the room, "What do you have for me Matt?"

"Interestingly, your father opened this account in an era of high interest rates and with the power of compounding; the value of the account is $750,000. You and your mother are the listed beneficiaries so the process of payout would be simple and I can help you facilitate that. I have the form in electronic format and can send it to you now."

"*I was not expecting anything like that*," he said sitting in a chair to gather himself. "I thought it would be enough to help my mom and take the pressure of finances off of us. *That will do much more*," he said with a voice of great relief and emotion.

"I am truly glad to hear that this solves so many problems for you and your mother. I can handle this for you but a large amount such as this requires a comprehensive plan to maximize its impact to both your lives."

"Of course," affirmed Mr. Branch, "The needs I just mentioned would only take about $150,000 and I would want the other money to generate income for my mom and then set up a program for me to take care of my family -"

"The way your father just took care of you with Generational Wealth. I would love to assist helping you develop that plan. For now, let's begin the process of getting you this money. I will have my assistant, Anna, set something up for us to get back together to discuss a financial plan once the payout has been made."

He said "*my assistant*" before he even thought of it. Just as Mr. Branch was adjusting to an instant life change, Matt knew that he was making them as well - *all leading him to a new level of higher results.*

Calling in the big guns

The day had been a whirlwind and Matt still had one more appointment. It was just a few minutes prior to 4:30pm as Matt rang the doorbell of a very nice home in one of the more prominent neighborhoods in the city. "Good afternoon Mrs. Clemmons, my name is Matt and I am here for our 4:30pm appointment."

"Actually, it is Ms. Clemmons, and I have a host of questions for you regarding your company and the services you offer. Come in and let's meet in the study. I have all my other papers arranged on my desk."

As they entered the study, Matt was shocked at the amount of financial literature that was neatly laid out on the desk. It was obvious that she had been doing an exhaustive amount of research. He also caught a glimpse of her JD Law degree from Fulbright. His intuition kicked in and this time he didn't think it prudent to rush into establishing the commonality of their alma mater. She didn't seem like the small talk type and he wanted to avoid what might be viewed as the classic salesman's approach.

"I can see you have done an extensive review of financial products. I am familiar with most of these companies and their offerings. What goals are you trying to achieve?" asked Matt surmising that the direct approach was best.

"Well, I hope that the competitive bid approach I am taking doesn't put you off," she stated unemotionally. "I am empowering myself to do what is best for me in an area that is not my expertise - finances - but is vitally important, so I have made a study of it. For the moment, the goals I have are secondary. I have specific products I would like to discuss with you and then have you conduct a detailed analysis of your offerings against those of your competitors."

"That seems like a valid approach and I would be more than happy to provide you the specific details of our products, but I may not be in the best position to relay the benefits of the competitors programs," he said candidly. He had just gotten comfortable with his own products.

"Ok Matt, I will throw you a bone. I have sat through about 4 of these meetings and countless seminars. I chose you to go *last* because of your company rating, reputation and the client reviews I have researched online. *Going last is giving you a distinct advantage.* No need to dazzle me, but simply provide the most comprehensive information in the format I requested and I think we can do business. The last hint about my seriousness is that I have assets that qualify me as a HNWI - High Net-Worth Individual. Does that help your *motivation* to take on this project?"

Matt loved the direct approach of Ms. Clemmons, but began to be troubled by his ability to perform at the level of her request. *What would LeRoy say?* "Rise above the burger wars and only represent your products?" *What about his father?* "If you give your best and fail you have no reason to be disappointed?" *What about Grandbooty?* "Have the faith in yourself to fight lions and move mountains?" *What would Larry say?* "If you aren't the right messenger and you can't deliver the right message...find someone who can - don't lose the sale!" In the end, he decided to use an amalgamation of them all;

"Ms. Clemons, my true motivation is to help you in a way that is most beneficial to you, your goals, and preserving the positive image you have of our company. Based on what you have shared, my fiduciary responsibility to you and my company is to refer you to Larry Wilcox. He is the top advisor in our region and specializes in High Net-Worth Individuals such as you. His client reputation is stellar and he can conduct the competitive review with explicit details on product variances and help you make an objective decision."

"Refreshing," she exclaimed, "A broker who didn't go 'gaga' over my resources or earning a commission - which by the way *you would earn* by my exacting nature. Actually, I have a colleague who is a client of Larry's and I was looking for someone to give me concentrated individual attention as opposed to just being another big account."

"No cause for concern, as Larry is the most efficient and hands-on person I know. Also, you don't get rid of me that easily! I would provide assistance to him and would be your primary contact as we earn your business. *Besides, we Fulbright alumni have to stick together.* I received my finance degree two years ago," said Matt sensing an opportunity build genuine rapport.

"Ah...holding the real evidence for the closing argument," she said smiling for the first time. "A favored tactic in my law practice. I have a few years on you from Fulbright and I have done well with my practice. I want to provide for a comfortable and early retirement," she admitted becoming more at ease.

"An early retirement to an exotic island or a long sabbatical in the Paris countryside?" Matt assumed.

"Nothing quite that romantic. My true love is children and I would love to teach elementary school the 2nd half of my life with no concern of finances. Yes, I can do Paris during the summer breaks," her demeanor now one of a person envisioning their future.

"Noble and doable," said Matt quoting something he remembered LeRoy saying to him about his goals in life. "My wife is a kindergarten teacher and while you are correct the economic benefits don't align with the value of the work, *she loves each and every minute of it.* If agreeable, I would like to reach out to Larry and introduce you to him."

With her affirming head nod, he dials the number at work and Larry's assistant answers the phone. "Good afternoon, this is Matt, is Larry available?"

"Yes he is, one moment Matt," his assistant answers as if she talks to him often.

"Mr. Palmer, what surprise do you have for me now?" Larry answered feigning annoyance.

"I am here with a perspective client Ms. Doris Clemmons, Esq. and I would like to introduce you to her for an analysis she wants completed. May I put you on speaker?"

"Of course...how are you today Ms. Clemmons?"

"Your junior associate has done an admirable job of turning me over to the big guns. No offense Matt."

"None taken - and yes, I knew I was overmatched!" he said laughing.

"Mr. Wilcox, I believe we have a mutual acquaintance," she said coyly.

"That would be attorney Derek Johnston and that would make you the Clemmons in Johnston, Clemmons and Jacobson. Congratulations on your recent ruling on the Hornsby case - a brilliant piece of litigation."

"Impressive. I see you read the funny papers."

"Nothing funny about the way you defend the defenseless. I would love to discuss your goals...of course with the highest level of discretion," Larry sensing the need to confirm a mutual understanding of propriety.

"Yes, attorney-client privilege would be critical. I love my partners, but they may not understand all of my goals beyond the interest of the practice. What would be the odds of meeting two sales people of integrity in one day? *There is a joke in there somewhere.*"

"Have you heard the one about the lawyer and the sales person?" Matt began.

"Let's not get *too familiar*," jested Ms. Clemmons. "Ok Mr. Wilcox, when can you meet?"

Act III - Shop Talk

Chasing windmills...finding windfalls

It was Tuesday morning and Matt was in attendance at the weekly meeting at Daniel's barbershop. He sat quietly in the back while they wrapped up their business discussions, which were filled with tangential conversations and people texting and using their tablets. There was little interest in the meeting but they were all certainly enjoying the ham and cheese croissants that he had brought in, smacking between jokes. It was all the typical barbershop scene - they were good guys, just not very serious. Daniel walked up front to introduce him.

"Ok, guys, I want to introduce Matt who is going to help us get our finances in order. Matt, come on up and tell us what you have," said Daniel off the cuff.

Matt hands out a one-page summary of the things that he can do to help them protect, preserve and create wealth. He had purposefully condensed the material into a simple, but interest-piquing format. It didn't really seem to matter as some were only paying cursory attention, and others were getting ready for the day. Unfazed by the apparent lack of interest, he continues to speak as planned; asking questions and answering questions for those that asked them. He could tell that Daniel was a little more than embarrassed with the lack of attention.

"Hey Matt, don't worry about these clowns - they prefer to have their 'money funny'. *I still need your help*," he reassured.

"No worries, I am just glad you let me come today. As for you, the next barbershop mogul, I would be honored to help you," Matt said unfazed by the last 20 minutes.

Just then a man and woman walk in and asked, "*Is the meeting over, are we too late?*"

"What's up E?" saluted Daniel with a fist bump and man hug. "This is Matt, the Generational Wealth Specialist I was telling you about. This is Ernest Simons, one of the barbers and his wife Connie."

"Good to meet you Mr. and Mrs. Simons - and you are never too late...I am here for you," said Matt shaking their hands.

"Can we talk in private?" asked Ernest in a whisper.

"You can use the back room where we keep the supplies, if that is ok," said Daniel.

They entered the cluttered room but the informality was actually good enough. It was obvious they had something important to ask that they didn't want the others to hear.

"A few weeks ago Connie lost her grandfather," began Ernest.

"I am truly sorry to hear that," said Matt sympathetically.

"Yes, we were very close," said Connie fighting back tears. "I was his only grandchild and he left me some land in the country along with a house. We just had it appraised and the value was over $550,000."

"It is in a prime business spot and even with the real estate environment the lawyer told us we should not have trouble finding a buyer. After commissions and everything else, we expect to have $500,000 cash. We have never seen that kind of money before and we don't know what to do," Ernest admitted candidly.

"It is a lot of money...*what do you want to do?* Matt inquired.

"We have had our eye on a new luxury car and want to add on to our small house. Now we can afford to have kids," said Ernest.

"Those things sound great. I am fortunate my grandfather, we call him Grandbooty, is still alive, but he did something like that for me once. *What do you think your grandfather would want you to do?*" he asked getting them to think deeper about the potential of this windfall.

"*If you don't mind me asking, what did your grandfather give you?*" asked Connie intently.

"*My future* - a college education that has given me this career...*my business*. I never met your grandfather but assume I took him a lifetime to acquire what he just gave you. You owe it to him to make it work for lifetime - *to use it to grow*," he said speaking from experience.

"That makes sense. I want to honor him, his memory and his gift by making it more than it is today. He was born in the heart of the Civil Rights struggle and was one of the first African Americans to own his home in this town. He was very proud of it," Connie relayed now in full tears.

"Bless your heart. I can see what he meant to you. When I was in kindergarten, I gave my mom a small rose plant. She has it in the yard right now...*20 years later*. Each day that he cares for it, she is reminded of me. That is what we will do with this blessing from your grandfather. Protect both of your futures, preserve an amount of the wealth for contingencies, and grow the rest so that it can help you leave a legacy for your kids - *Generational Wealth*. Each new financial pillar we create will be a testament to his gift."

"Yes, buying a new car *can wait*," said Ernest in support of Matt's rationale.

"You may have to delay gratification for a while, but keep thinking big. Determine *what* you want out of life, *why* you want it and *how* you will achieve it always emerges!" Matt said passionately. "Your grandfather has just given you a big leg up in your lives and now life is providing you answers on how to get where you want to be." He silently thought about the trail of crumbs that Grandbooty had talked about.

"Speaking of how...how do we get started?" asked Connie

"Let me do a little leg work to see the best approach. I also think I have a real estate agent for you to help you sell the house for the best terms. I will be in touch on Monday to give you next steps. *For now, rest assured that we will do all the right things to give you a bright future,*" he said confidently.

Matt realized that his job gave him great power and responsibility to impact futures. Mr. Jacob's was just the beginning and as long as he had people's best interest at heart, he would receive the three-fold blessing that LeRoy had taught him - *emancipation, gratification and remuneration.* At the moment, gratification was most important and as LeRoy had commanded as a requirement of the profession...*he was beginning to love what he did!*

Making dollars with common cents

A s Matt wrapped up the discussion with the Simons, Daniel came back to the storage room with two of the other barbers. "I see you have turned this into an office. Maybe we should charge you rent!" laughed Daniel. "These are my boys Bobby and Clarence. We are a little more serious than the rest. Speaking of rent, we are ready to stop paying it and start earning some by charging it...*how do we do it?*"

"Besides coming to your establishment for a great haircut, I don't know much about this business. Give me an idea of how it works for you today," Matt queried.

"We pay the owner rent and other shared expenses, and we keep the rest," said Clarence.

"Yea, it is a sweet deal for the owner," added Bobby. "It is time for us to get paid, and we have the mind for this business."

"*That will be your most valuable asset,*" replied Matt supportive of his statement. "When you don't have all the resources you need you have to have the right mindset. You will need to engage innovation and ingenuity - that will always make up the difference generating resourcefullness. Speaking of resources, how much money do you have for your business?"

"We have $1,500 each and can put in $500 a month into whatever we do. The $500 is what we pay the owner now to be in his shop," said Daniel slapping Clarence "five" over what they had amassed.

"Great start! What about a building or space for your new establishment?"

"That's just it...no bank will give us a loan even though we have 25 years of barber experience between us, and we have 12 barbers in the wings to start the shop. We want to have a more upscale shop...uptown," boasted Bobby.

"What if you could find a building that didn't require you to purchase it, but instead lease it with a monthly rate or lease-purchase it. The market uptown is soft and I am sure there are people who will work with you."

"Now that makes sense," said Daniel. I know that the owner here pays about $2,000 a month all in. If we could get a place for the same amount and charge our barbers $500 a month when we would clear $4,000 a month!"

"Can you help us with that?" asked Clarence.

"That is not my direct area of expertise, but I can make some calls and refer you to the right people," said Matt confident in his small but growing network of professionals.

"*What will you get out of the deal?*" asked Daniel. "We can't have you changing our lives and walking away empty-handed."

"Once we get you guys up and running, you will need to establish a formal business agreement and best-practice is to obtain forms of business protection and preservation that I can help you with. Also, since this will be an upscale operation, you will want to make benefits and wealth-building programs available to your barbers, too. Moreover, when you have 10 shops and are wealthy, I want to be your money manager for life...your Generational Wealth Specialist."

"Matt, I think I can speak for Clarence and Bobby," began Daniel, "You are a good guy with great ideas and are willing to work with us from the beginning....*when we are small with big dreams.*"

"I have admitted to you that I am new as well," he confessed. "We can grow together. One day we will look back on the humble beginning in this storage room and tell our children this is where greatness was born!"

Introducing my good friend...

Matt made his way over the Rotary Club where Mr. Jacobs had arranged for him to speak at their monthly luncheon meeting. Mr. Jacobs meets him at the door with a handshake and warm embrace.

"Good to see you Matt, I am glad that you could make it," he said warmly. "I will take you around to introduce you to a few influential men and good friends. The real purpose of these meetings is to eat lunch and hobnob. I would advise you not to talk too long...no more than 10 minutes."

Matt was glad for the heads up and quickly cancelled his idea of a 20 minute PowerPoint presentation and 10 minute Q&A. The shift in timing was a minor point, as he appreciated the opportunity to speak to so many people all at once. He likened this to making 100 cold calls and if you got 3 appointments out of it, you have played to the odds. *Surely there would be three people in the room that could become clients.*

As they walked around the room, it was evident that Mr. Jacobs was well respected and known by everyone. He had chaired several of the charitable initiatives and for the first time was heading up the committee for the annual golf outing. As they walked up to each person, Mr. Jacobs would introduce Matt and make a little jibe with each person. "Meet Matt Palmer, *my money man*, who will be speaking today. I know you are an old man with a short attention span but pay attention this time."

As they met another man he quipped "I haven't received your sponsor's registration for the golf tournament. Matt here is quite the golfer; maybe you could get him on your squad and give yourself a chance to win a prize for a change!"

Each interaction brought hugs and clamorous laughter as these men had a genuine affinity and respect for each other. It was almost time for the meeting to begin, and Mr. Jacobs whispered to Matt about a man he had to meet...Mr. Robert Baker.

"Bob, I would like you to meet Matt Palmer, my money man. Matt, this old coot has more grandchildren and great grandchildren than he can name." He whispers to Matt again, "*He also has more money than he knows what to do with - sharp as Warren Buffet, but can't hear worth nothing*". He then yells to Mr. Baker, "Either sit up close or turn up your hearing aid so you can hear what this man has to say - I would put him up against any of your money men," Mr. Jacobs bragged.

"Son, if you are friends with this old codger Jacobs, then you might not be so trustworthy - *a man is known for the company he keeps*," said Mr. Baker with a raucous belly laugh and slapping Mr. Jacobs on the back like the oldest of friends.

"Looks like they are just about ready to start. Matt, I will introduce you and then you can address the group."

"I am ready," said Matt aloud. "At least I think I am ready," he says under his breath to himself.

"Good afternoon gentlemen and I do use the term loosely! Today we are in for a real treat and I don't mean the banana pudding for dessert! You will all have to hold your appetites for a few more minutes and give this young man your full attention. He is talking about a topic that is most important for all of us. No, he is not a doctor here to talk to you about your prostate or your touch of arthritis...*he is here to talk about your money.* As many of you know, I am a somewhat stubborn man (chorus of 'no's' emanate from the crowd), but this young man knocked on my door and changed my life. He has set me up a program that will allow me to enjoy my golden years, and leave a legacy for my children's children. I give thanks that most of us in this room are blessed with good health, strength, ample minds - *most of you anyway.* Even though times have changed and been a little rough; most of us are also blessed with the finances that allow us to take care of our families and serve our communities. We have to be good stewards over what the good Lord has given (*audible amen's abound*). I have no doubt that if you give this young man a hearing ear and open heart he can do the same thing for you as he has done for me. Without further delay, I am proud to introduce Matthew Palmer, Generational Wealth Specialist and my good friend." He shakes Matt's hand and hugs him warmly giving him the microphone.

"Thank you Mr. Jacobs. Good afternoon to all of you. I truly appreciate the opportunity to speak to you today but also appreciate the fact that all that is standing between you and banana pudding is me! (Laughter from the group). If you give me a few minutes of attention, I promise not to be too long (a chorus of 'here here's' sparsely from the crowd)

Matt reaches into his pocket and pulls out some coins. He rattles it around in his hand then holds it up to his ear to hear the sound. He opens his palm showing the copper and silver coins out for all to see. In my hand, I have 36 cents of loose change. **Everybody say Change!** (A few people comply) Let me ask this group...*what can I do with this change today?*

"A pack of gum," shouts one man.

"A phone call - *if* you can find a working phone booth," yells another.

"10 minutes on the city parking meter and you better not be late coming back! Fred, the police chief over here needs the revenue from the ticket he will give you!" There is laughter throughout the hall.

"All great answers. Truth is you really can't do much with this today," Matt inserts. "What could you do with it 50 years ago? 75 years ago?"

"I remember my dad talking about the depression and people asking '*Brother can you spare a dime?*' Back then 36 cents could buy you a sandwich and a cup of coffee," one man remarked to a chorus of 'ain't that the truth' from the crowd.

"I used to go to the corner store and get my grandmother a loaf of bread, and myself a nickel coke and 3 cents worth of cookies - *even had change to give her back!*"

"Wouldn't that make you Methuselah?" cat called another man.

"There is no doubt that 36 cents was worth something *back in the day. What happened to this change?*" asked Matt ready to bring the first point home. "The answer in fancy economic terms *is inflation.* Inflation doesn't mean your money isn't valuable, but it has lost some of its punch. The first thing your money has to do is keep up with inflation so the dollar you have today will still *feel* like a dollar tomorrow. That means your money needs to *grow* to keep pace with inflation. *How do you get your money to grow?*"

"With all the chaos of the day, I say put it under your pillow and pray that the tooth fairly won't steal it!" said a man up front.

"No worries there! Most of you old coots don't have your real teeth anyway!" shouted the class clown from earlier. "My vote is to dig a hole out back and bury it for a better day!"

Matt spoke quickly to regain control and keep on his impromptu message. "In some respects, both of those comical responses are about the same as putting your money in U.S. Treasuries that are currently paying little or nothing."

"Yes, but at least there my money is safe!" exclaimed a man from the back of the room.

"Give that man a gold star!" replied Matt. "The real challenge people have is growing their money - but not growing their anxiety and sleepless nights! (Amen's) So making money grow has risks...right? *Does anyone remember the economic environment during Jimmy Carter's presidency?*

"Long gas lines and higher prices!" said one man.

"Correct! Can anyone tell me the interest rates on CDs back then?" Matt queried the room.

"Over 15%!" many of them chorused.

"What is it now?" asked Matt now in rapid fire mode with increasing participation from the room.

"Essentially nothing!" said a growing crescendo of people in the room.

"But the stock market is at an all time high, *right?* So somebody is making money, *right? How are they doing it?* They have adapted to change...someone shout *Change!*" This time, the majority of the room joined in. He had gained their full attention with his call and response approach commanding the floor like Jack Jeffries had done a couple of weeks back.

"I am sure most of you remember your parents talking about huddling round the radio for their favorite show. Despite being The Great Depression, the price of radios came down sharply and people found a way to afford them. *Remember?* (Hands went up all over the room) To demonstrate the impact of change, just 60 years ago, only some of you post World War II baby boomers had phones or televisions in your homes. Fast forward and now *all of you* have big screen TV's, cell phones in your pockets, computers in your home and now the internet. Right now, I could make a video of this meeting, post it on You Tube and millions around the world could see it - *all in minutes and from this little phone that I hold in my hand.* Everybody shout *Change!*" This time the entire room exploded.

Matt continued at a controlled but enthusiastic pace, "The opportunities for growing your money while managing risk *have evolved.* But if you still look for 36 cents to buy you a sandwich and coffee you, will be continue to be disappointed...and your money will continue lose its buying power."

"How do we keep pace with inflation?" came a question from the center of the room.

"I am glad you asked," said Matt ready to release his solution. "What do I hold in this hand" (shaking the coins) - *Change!* What do I have in the other hand" (holding up the smart phone) - *Change!* As a generational wealth specialist, my goal and job is to help you develop a plan that will provide, protect and preserve your hard earned assets - all the while keeping up with *changing environments* and *evolving opportunities.* I know that many of you already have trusted financial advisors, and I am not here today to change that relationship. There are some of you that need help with *the change* I have outlined and will be ready to take the next step. *It is those people I believe I can help the most."*

Just then a man stands up in the audience. "Let me vouch for this young man. Matt here is helping me and Beverly with stabilizing our retirement. He even got our nay-saying son over the hump of cynicism. True, we are just getting started with him, but I can vouch for his client focused approach."

Matt recognized him from the day before. "It is great to see you again Mr. Francis and thank you for those supportive words," Matt not believing the smallness of the community.

Others raised their hand to ask questions, but the 10 minutes was just about up. Mr. Jacobs walked up to the front of the room. "No more complimentary advice for you free-loaders. Matt here is a professional and would be more than happy to talk to you during lunch or in a private meeting. His cards and brochures are on this table and you can get them as you get your food. Let's show Matt our appreciation for his spot on speech"

The crowd all stood to their feet and gave him sincere applause. Matt felt great as he had spoken extemporaneously to address the genre of the crowd. All of the history lessons and finance courses at Fulbright had made it feel easy, unforced and natural. He didn't know if he would get any clients, but he felt good about his second speaking performance for the day.

A man of few words

Matt was saying good bye to Mr. Jacobs in the parking lot when an older gentlemen walked up to them. It was Mr. Baker who he had gotten introduced to earlier. "Young man, do you have a few minutes?" he asked politely.

"Of course Mr. Baker," replied Matt. "Mr. Jacobs, I will be in touch you with later this week and thank you for everything!" They shook hands and Mr. Jacobs entered his car leaving Matt and Mr. Baker standing in the parking lot.

"Don't know if you can tell, but I am a little hard of hearing," began Mr. Baker. "Makes me talk too loud and I don't want anyone to know all of my business."

"I can appreciate that," Matt answered empathetically, "Money is a very important but personal topic. *What can I do to help you?*"

"Well, honestly, I didn't hear everything that you said up there but if Mr. Jacobs says you are a good man and one to be trusted, that is enough for me. He is not easily won over...*nether am I*. Guess the result of being an old man that has seen a little of everything."

"I prefer to call it sage wisdom! I will do whatever I can for you based on your goals and desires."

"I am getting on in years, and I have built up some pretty good holdings. Most of it is in blue chips and other strong companies. Recently, many of them have struggled and I need to begin moving some of my money into safer, more predictable vehicles. I am not focused as much on return as I am preserving my money for future generations. I see on your business card that you specialize in helping people do that."

"Yes sir, my company has a series of programs and products that can help you achieve those goals," began Matt. "*When would you like to get together for us to review your situation and begin building a plan?*"

"I would rather you speak with my attorney who handles everything for me. He manages the various trusts for my family and my charities. His name is Alan Weiss. Let me call him now to introduce you," he says already dialing the phone. "Hey Alan, I want you to speak to this young man named Matt. I want to do business with him for some of the funds we are transferring...here he is," said Mr. Baker handing Matt the phone.

"Good afternoon Mr. Weiss, this is Matt Palmer -"

"Good fortune had smiled on you if you have found favor with Mr. Baker. He is *very* exacting as it relates to the integrity of his brokers. As he outlined, I handle all of his affairs and trusts. We are looking for various insurance products to stabilize his vast portfolio and I am in the midst of due diligence. Give me the two minute overview of your company," Mr. Weiss said directly and businesslike.

Matt begins to relay some key features of his company and core products. Based on questions and responses it was evident that Mr. Weiss had done this a time or two.

"Ok, Matt - I have what I need for now. I am familiar with your company and actually need someone to assist me with products with your firm for other clients. If all goes well, maybe we can set up a mutually beneficial client referral relationship. For now, the fact that Mr. Baker likes you is enough. *However, to get the business, I have to like the products, your service and the measurable results.* Fair enough? Give me your email address and I will be in touch."

Matt gave him all the contact information and handed the phone back to Mr. Baker, "Thanks Alan...keep me posted."

Matt walked him to his car and no additional words were exchanged. Matt didn't even attempt more small talk. When they arrived at his car, Mr. Baker shakes his hand and simply says goodbye. Matt walks back to his car understanding that prospects come in all shapes, sizes, and personalities. He has to take each person at the face value of their interaction. No longer could fall into the trap of prejudging what people need, why they need it or if they will buy. *He will simply tell his story everywhere he goes.* As LeRoy used to say you should be like a politician on the stump - 'shaking hands and kissing babies'...and then wait for the votes to come in. Matt has certainly increased his level of activity and he could feel great things coming his way!

Act IV - The Evans Agency Project

The supporting cast

I t was Wednesday morning and Matt was anticipating another very eventful day; he was meeting with David first thing, there was a meeting for the initial planning for the Evans Agency account and follow-up on all the activities from the last couple of days. Thankfully, his new assistant, Anna Jones, was also coming in at 8:00am. *Yes, it was going to be a busy day.*

"Good morning Matt," said David with a big smile on his face holding yet another contract in his hand. "*Is this what it feels like to be successful?* I could get used to this!"

"Another good day, I surmise?"

"You would surmise correctly. Between Monday and yesterday, I have 4 new contracts to report. I have to tell you, it feels good. I finally believe I have found my *sales voice* that they talked about in the E^4 program.

"So what is *your voice*?" asked Matt curiously.

"Not to try to be someone I am not. I can't use some of the hard driving closes or unnatural banter - *at least unnatural to me*. I know everyone has their own way but I now realize that mine is to leverage my operational prowess. Once I actually get into the home and can hear what they need the right product just '*appears*' in my mind. Then I know how to explain it in a way that is simple to understand. So far, I haven't even had to fight big objections because they see the answer as clearly as I do," he declared triumphantly.

"I am so happy for your success, and more importantly, *finding your voice*," Matt said sincerely. "Speaking of which, what you just said is exactly why I wanted you to come in this morning. I need your operational skills to help me with the Evans Agency account."

"*My help*...what about Larry?" asked David incredulous with the request.

"There is no doubt that Larry is the best and will help get to the heart of the buying decision. By his own admission, he leverages the operations team's expertise for large and more complex accounts to ensure a smooth implementation. In the 5 minute call with Bret yesterday, I realized that I could leverage the company's best operational voice for this account - *you*. I also realize that by constructing a team, we can do more and get more business. Besides, it would mean 20% commission for you if we close the deal."

"*Why didn't you say that to begin with?* Count me in!"

"Matt, you have a guest at the front," said a voice over the intercom.

"That will be my new assistant Anna," said Matt proudly.

"*Assistant?*" remarked Suzy who had just walked up to her desk with Brad right behind. "It's about time you got someone to organize your life and affairs. With the new baby on the way, leveraging time will become even more important...*good for you!*"

Matt took Anna back to one of the meeting rooms to discuss the game plan and get to know her better. "Since you have supported top sales people for the company before, I will lean on you to help me establish what you know to be best practices. *I am not ashamed to tell you that I am still finding my way,*" Matt admitted.

"Make no mistake; even though I have a variety of successful experiences, *I will be working for you.* My main assignment is to make *your life* easier through efficiency, free up your time to make more sales to generate revenue and reinforce your trusted advisor status with each client interaction. I have to tell you, it feels good to be back in the sales environment. I love the fast-paced nature of it and ensuring that clients get the highest level of service," said Anna making her case.

"In that way, I think we will provide synergy for each other. I am beginning to have a lot of things happen and they are already running together," Matt conceded he had reached a sticking point of capacity.

"Might I suggest our communication strategy?" asked Anna before proceeding.

"Yes, whatever you think will be the most efficient."

"I have an internet based virtual assistant program tied to my cell phone," initiated Anna. "When you have tasks that you need me to accomplish, you simply call the number, dictate what you need and then I will complete the task. Until I build familiarity with your clients, I will need a few more particulars, but eventually, you will only need a few words to instruct me. Over time, I will intuitively know much of what needs to happen for each client without you asking."

"What about using email to send you tasks?" asked Matt thinking that would be efficient.

"If you type me an email of instruction, you might as well have handled it yourself. *How many words do you type a minute?*" she answered with a wink.

"Do I have to answer than? I definitely *talk* faster than I *type!*" he said laughing.

"We have to be efficient in everything we do and you will be off-loading the tedious tasks to me. I like to call them 'menial but meaningful' tasks. We also need to use the company's cloud-based SharePoint site that lets me access your Calendar, contacts, important files, and most importantly, sync your emails. That will allow me to send emails on your behalf after you tell me the nature of your correspondence -"

"Using the virtual assistant where I can simply speak the instructions!" interjected Matt as he started to see the good organization of a consolidated platform of interactions.

"Exactly! To get us started, I need to enter all of your leads into the contact relationship management program, called a CRM, and then show you how to do real time dispositions for your call outcomes. I will create a series of drop downs so you don't have to type anything in - simply drop down the menu and choose the best outcome. Once a week, I will run a report that show how effective your phone time is and the close rate for appointments...by source."

"That all sounds very familiar. My colleagues and I just went through the E⁴ Boot camp and much of what you are saying was covered there," Matt's mind filled with new revelation of how the program's roadmap was iterative and progressive.

"Yes, I am familiar with the program since the last sales rep I worked for went through it and implemented much of the program," acknowledged Anna. "It was very well laid out and effective - we can continue to use that as our roadmap. *Finally, we need to put together the proposal for the Evan's Agency.*"

"We are meeting this morning with David and Larry to go over the game plan. I have my first meeting with the HR person at the agency tomorrow at 1pm if you can make it?"

"Yes, I can do that. As for my ongoing schedule, I can do most of the things I mentioned *virtually* using technology. I can come into the office twice a week on Mondays and Wednesdays, but would be available by phone all other times. Once the evaluation period of one week is over, we can more clearly define our schedules" Anna reminding him of their original deal.

"About that...I can already see the value of all you know, your experiences and how you can help me build my business. I crunched the numbers and if agreeable I would like to procure your services on an independent contractor basis to start...and then, I want you to grow as I grow. Here is an initial payment outline for you to review. You can take the week to review and give me your decision," Matt summarized.

"Very professional...*looks like something your new assistant might do?*" Anna said laughing. "I am sure all is in order and I look forward to a long and mutually prosperous relationship."

When a plan comes together

At 7:55am Matt wrapped things up with Anna so they wouldn't be late for the planning with Larry and his assistant for the Evans Agency account. He grabbed David on the way to his office. "*Did you tell Larry that you were bringing me on board for this shindig?*" David asked timidly. "He doesn't strike me as the kind of guy that likes surprises, *or too many hands.*"

Matt realizes that he hasn't, but he also knew that Larry expected him to do the heavy lifting on the account...especially based on their 70/30 colleague split.

"Good morning Anna...great to see you again," said Larry hugging her. "You look terrific! How is your husband, John, and little Jonathon?"

"They are doing wonderful. He is adjusting to his new job, I am adapting to a new city and Jonathon is simply *amazing*. Lots of change but I think things will work out now that I have joined forces with Matt."

"Good morning Mr. David, *can I help you?*" asked Larry in a feigned agitated tone.

"Actually, I asked David to be a part of our team. There is no one better at implementation and product knowledge so I thought it wise to include him from the onset," Matt declared boldly.

"This is your show Matt, but I agree with your decision-making. I have worked with David before and from an operational standpoint he will be an asset, but from a sales standpoint - ."

"*Are you trying to say my sales skill is somewhat lacking? My 4 sales would prove you different?*" David said proudly.

"Congratulations," said Larry sincerely and shaking his hand. "As for this rodeo, *we will need you to do what you do best.* That goes for all of us. A primary client concern will be the efficiency of transition. Realize it is harder to move a client who is already engrained with another company. Not only do we have to be better, we have to move them past their natural inclination to leave things as they are. They have not expressed unhappiness with their current company so we have our work cut out for us."

"But remember - Mrs. Evans digs The Messenger," said Matt playfully.

"That goodwill only got you to Ms. Hicks, who is tougher than nails. The frat-boy charm will be lost on her. We have to leverage our unique sales proposition and do it in such a way that makes us the obvious choice. Ok Matt, how do we go after this account?"

"Here is the timeline and particulars as we know them; I have a meeting with the office and HR manager, Leanne Simpson tomorrow at 1pm. Anna will accompany me to organize the demographics and input the data. We should have direct access to the 30 direct employees and email access to the 1,000 independent representatives. We meet to do the final presentation next Friday at 10am - Ms. Hicks chose that day," said Matt in concession of Larry's normal day off.

"A Friday presentation for this account is a small price to pay," supported Larry with a smile.

"What approach do you think we can take to provide the unique sales proposition?" asked David. "I assume it will be predicated on one of your off the wall metaphors or analogies."

"That's it! When I met Mr. and Mrs. Evans at La Dulce Vita, I referred to helping her build her business using a Happy People Program."

"Acronyms and smiley faces won't get her intrigued enough to move her business," Larry remarked unimpressed.

"As you astutely mentioned, neither Mrs. Evans nor Ms. Hicks *feel enough pain* to make our proposition easy. However, what if we could demonstrate that *their staff and agents* weren't totally satisfied or that they desired additional options? The kind of options that *our program*s could provide - that might create the leverage we need."

"Now you are getting somewhere," said Larry.

"I have a suggestion," interjected Anna.

"By all means, I want *every voice* in the room to be heard," answered Matt.

"In California, we conducted blind surveys as a precurser to a proposal. The data gathered can be used to demonstrate a need that they might not know exists."

"Of course the data might show that they are *all happy* and we would be sunk," lamented David.

"If we simply go in with products, even competitively priced, without the leverage of client dissatisfaction, we will be 'sunk' anyway," commented Larry. "I like the simple concept if undergirded by hard data from their teams."

"Time draws nigh and a survey sounds ambitious. *How can we pull that off?*" asked Matt directing his attention to Anna who had gone to the whiteboard to outline the process.

"Since there are only 30 employees, we can conduct a confidential survey by phone," she explains. "Since it will be official company business, we can make it mandatory for them. For the independent agents, I can set up an electronic survey with no problem. To make it statistically relevant we would need at least 10% participation. The only way to garner that response rate is by offering a gift for their participation. We can systemically limit the gift expense to the first 100 so we don't incur more costs than necessary. "

"We have done those before for client satisfaction polls," added David. "We offered a $10 lunch certificate at a good local eatery. The restaurant would then offer them a ½ off special that could be purchased for that certificate price (value $20). I can call Bret, as I think they just did one in the area and we could piggy back on it."

"These are great ideas and I think the right approach," Matt confirmed. For the first time in a long while, he didn't even focus on the money it would cost. He knew the investment would pay off. *Larry, what do you think?*"

"Execution will be critical and we have to go in polished and ready to take on the natural questions that will arise. *We also need the data to support our assertions.* That is the main risk, but I think a calculated one that we need to take."

"Regarding execution; Anna, you will be responsible for the telephonic and electronic survey questions template. You will also accompany me tomorrow to gather the proper demographic data - *make sure I don't miss anything* - we won't have time for a redo," directed Matt.

"I have done this dozens of times," replied Anna confidently. "I am ready and this is exciting!"

"David, get Anna and Bret together for the electronic survey gift coordination. Also, once I get the information on their current plan, I need you to do an operational SWOT analysis. Nothing too in-depth since my goal is not to make the other company look bad, but I need to know their strengths, weaknesses, opportunities, and threats just in case."

"Got it captain!" saluted David.

"Larry, I was hoping that you would take lead on determining best mix of products and delivering that portion of the presentation - that is your strength."

"I already have ideas based on the last 5 years of chasing this account...I will be ready," confirmed Larry.

"Finally, I will conduct the 30 telephonic interviews with the employed staff. I will also prepare the executive summary and opening for the proposal. Let's all meet again next Wednesday morning to review our findings and have a final meeting on Thursday for a run through of Friday's presentation".

"Putting it on everyone's calendar as we speak," Anna relayed typing quickly on her laptop.

"I love it when a plan comes together," said a satisfied Matt. "Thank all of you for your gifts and talents. *That is what will give us our best chance of success.* I don't see how we can lose with the stuff we use!"

The Preliminaries

Matt and Anna were at the Evans Agency office at 12:45am and were waiting in the reception area for the meeting with Leanne Simpson. Since this was just discovery he felt confident that this portion would go smoothly. *Next week would be the real test.* As he looked around the lobby, he was amazed at all the awards, press clippings and photos with prominent people that graced the wall. Mrs. Evans was truly a leader who gave back to the community that had given her so much over the years.

"You must be Mr. Palmer," said a voice that he recognized from over the phone.

"Good afternoon Ms. Hicks," Matt said extending his hand. "This is my assistant Anna Jones."

"Good to meet you both, Leanne is just returning from lunch so it will be a few more minutes. Let me show you to her office," she said maintaining her 'business only' tone.

As they walked down a long corridor, there were even more pictures and awards. Matt knew better than to engage in small talk, but at that moment he remembered he had need of real estate agents.

"Ms. Hicks I have a couple of clients that need professional assistance with real estate. *Can you refer me to a couple of your best people?"*

"Certainly, what is the nature of their need?" she inquired.

"One of them is a free and clear property on State Street that should value about $550,000 for commercial use. The other client is looking for a barber shop location with flexible leasing terms. I can provide your agents with warm introduction to both clients."

"Excellent. As with any business, much of what we do comes from referrals. We also have frequent need of people in *your line of work* after clients secure properties. Let's see how the next couple of weeks transpire and we can look to establish a continuous symbiotic relationship. I will have Leanne provide you with two names. Thank you for thinking of us for your needs - it is appreciated," she said relaxing her tone slightly.

It was the first warm gesture that she had given him. Surely, she was cordial enough, but *all business* and reminded Matt of Larry. He also realized that what he did fit well with other professions such as real estate, lawyers, bankers, and others. Networking to the benefit of everyone would be an ideal way to secure clients.

"I need to develop a network of key professionals for mutual referrals," Matt whispered to Anna as they sat in Leanne's office. "I have a few people in mind, so remind me next week to begin a program."

Just then Leanne walked in breathing hard and extending her hand to both of them, "Sorry I am late - lunch with a client ran over."

"No worries Mrs. Simpson," said Matt, "Anna and I can give you some time to get your bearings. I can only imagine how busy you are and we are here for you."

"Please call me Leanne. You're too sweet Matt. Mrs. Evans said you were! I do need to make one quick call if I may...no need for you and Anna to leave. I am just checking in on my sitter who is watching my 1-year old" She placed the quick call and then turned her attention back to Matt and Anna.

"This must be a picture of your children?" asked Anna pointing to a large frame on her desk.

"Yes, I have been blessed with three of them. Angie and Barry are high school age and my little one just turned one. *Don't ask about the gap in ages...let's just say life is full of beautiful surprises.* It has almost been an epidemic in the office. We have 5 ladies who are expecting and 2 of the men's wives. *There must be something in the water!*"

"I just had my first one and Jonathon is not quite a year old," added Anna showing her a picture from her purse.

"My wife is due any day now," added Matt. "*There truly must be something in the water!*" They shared a good laugh and a few more minutes of small talk about children, the demand of parenthood and balancing careers.

"With all this talk about having children, how does it impact the office from a benefits standpoint?" Matt inquired making the logical transition to business.

"Admittedly, not all the expecting employees are happy," divulged Leanne. "As you would imagine, most of the administrative people are younger and at the point of starting families. So the only time they use the health benefits are for limited illness and pregnancies. *That is when the co-pay structure hits them.*"

"Your current program probably balances the benefits you offer with the premiums *they pay* and the part *you pay,*" he added to stimulate more discovery.

"Exactly. We have tried to strike the best balance possible in several areas while managing the cost of the programs - *costs have increased over the years but benefits seem flat.* What we have also tried to construct a progressive environment that allows them to strike the work-life equilibrium. Flexibility of schedules, ability to check in on kids and family oriented events. From a pure benefits perspective, we offer various insurance and savings vehicles. The participation is good, but I am not sure we are getting the mileage we need from them - the programs are essentially the same as 5 years ago. *I think times have changed...but we haven't.*"

Matt sensed this was the first opening to release his approach to their proposal. "What we had in mind to help you *measure* your employee satisfaction with their benefits program is to conduct a blind survey. This is Anna's area of expertise, so I will let her explain the process we would like to use."

Anna explains the program for the employed staff and the contracted agents. She masterfully outlines the process, showing Leanne the specific questions and how the internet-based program will compile the results for interpretation. Anna wrapped up the explanation when Leanne stood up from her chair.

"I love the idea and the process you have outlined," she said enthusiastically. "I have been considering some additional employee based programs but need more direct feedback before justifying the expense. *Can we make your employee survey more expansive to include some work program and environmental questions?*"

"Like a 360° review where they tell you what they like and dislike about the job, benefits and environment?" asked Matt.

"Exactly! While I know it may not be directly related to your purpose, *it would help me immensely.* I can draft a series of questions to add to yours. To save you time and effort, rather than have you call each person, I would schedule them to be at their computers on Monday from 9am-10am to complete the survey. *Would that work?*"

Matt realized that adding her questions vested her in the results. It also made his life much easier since he wouldn't have to make the 30 calls. Plus, all the data would be gathered and compiled for the employees 3 days ahead of schedule...it was a win-win.

"I think that is a masterful plan and will allow us to get the most out of the survey. The only remaining challenge is getting 100 of your agents to respond - *any ideas on maximizing their participation?*" Matt understanding she was now a champion for his cause.

"We see at least 30-40 agents every day coming in and out of the office. Based on the lunch certificate program Anna outlined, I think I can encourage those that come in the office to sit at a computer and answer the questions. My commitment to you is that 100 of them will have it completed by Wednesday. *Would that work?*"

"Perfect!" interjected Anna, "I would be in a position to share your employee results on Wednesday evening ahead of the presentation on Friday."

"Do you mind if we share that data with everyone on Friday?" asked Matt gaining permission to use her expanded questions as part of the official proposal.

"Of course," Leanne replied. "While my motives are somewhat selfish in that I want to develop new programs for the team, I understand that your presentation on Friday is your primary focus."

"If agreeable, I will review any revelations that emerge from the data with you first on Thursday so you have no surprises!" said Matt sealing their alliance.

"That would be ideal. *Who knows, you may actually make my job of pitching some new ideas to Mrs. Evans easier.*"

"Besides the other information that Anna can get from your employee handbook and benefit guides, I think we have all we need," said Matt. "Leanne, I truly thank you for your cooperation and I couldn't ask for a better outcome from today's meeting,"

"I agree and at the risk of going against the grain...*I am rooting for you.* I think a fresh new approach is what the agency needs to move into the next phase of our business growth and opportunity."

"Oh yes," began Anna, "We need two agent referrals for two of Matt's clients that need real estate expertise. I will send the particulars to you by email by end of day and you can send me your recommendations."

"*Keep sending referrals and I can tell you that today will only be the beginning of a great relationship!*" said Leanne exuberantly.

The Proposal

It was Wednesday morning and almost time for the scheduled meeting to go over the Evans Agency proposal. Matt was at his desk reviewing all his activity for the past few weeks. He had used the virtual office assistant program to dictate all the client interactions and required follow up activities to Anna. She had input them into his calendar with dates, times and alarms for him to prepare follow-up actions. She had even color coded his activity to denote prospective clients from those that were active. He was amazed at his client base and how it was growing. For weeks, it seemed like Mr. Jacobs was his *only client*, but now had close to a dozen...*and growing daily*.

"Good morning Mr. High Powered Sales Executive," said Suzy settling in her chair at the table. "You are giving me a run for my money on the leaderboard I see."

"You should have never told me all your secrets!"

"All kidding aside, it is great to see the success of you, David, and yes, even Brad over the last month. It just goes to show that when you mix the science of sales with artful elements, *success is assured*. I am very happy for you. How is the Evans account coming along?"

"We have meeting in a few minutes. Anna has gotten all of the data together from the survey and that will determine our approach. I haven't seen it yet...so fingers crossed," he said positively. Just then, Anna walked in the office and greeted Suzy and Matt. They gathered David and headed into Larry's office.

"Good morning all," began Matt, "This meeting is for us to go over the status of the Evans Agency account and develop the structure of the proposal. A few updates before I turn it over to Anna to share the data that I am yet to see. We had a great meeting with Leanne Simpson last Wednesday. She was very supportive and actually expanded the survey to include elements of employee job satisfaction along with benefit satisfaction. *No doubt that she is on our side.*"

"That is great news," asserted Larry, "You always have to have a champion on the inside - someone that sees the inherent need for change and believes you are the one to help them do it. Not that we want to pit her against Ms. Hicks and certainly not Mrs. Evans, but one more voice on our side never hurts.

"She was very instrumental in getting 100% compliance on the employee survey and successfully garnered 100 of the independent agents - all completed by yesterday which helped immensely," added Anna.

"David did a great job coordinating with Bret in operations regarding the lunch certificate program and integrating it seamlessly with Anna's effort. I am pleased to say that all has gone flawlessly up to this point. The real question now is - *how did the survey turn out?*" inquired Matt directing Anna to go up-front to share her results.

"Not to keep you in suspense, but I think the survey results play into our hands quite nicely in several ways." Anna passed out a series of papers with colored charts, graphs, and tables outlining the results. "Let's review the key findings and then the strategy for the proposal should emerge."

"Anna, this is impressive...*even by my standards.* I wonder who recommended you as a superstar assistant - oh...that would be me!" Larry said gloating.

"No doubt, I could not have done this without her!" confirmed Matt. "Just looking at the summary page, the results jump out at you. Overwhelmingly, the employees love their jobs at the agency with 89% satisfied or better. Yet, only 45% are satisfied with the benefits and programs offered.

"Even more telling is the customer service rating for the various programs," noted David. "*I am very familiar with the company they are using and service is not their strong suit.* To show immediate improvement in that area, we can implement a direct line task force assigned to the Evan's Agency."

"*What would that mean?*" asked Matt.

"It means that their calls would be routed to a special unit with an average speed of answer of 6 seconds and a 92% one call resolution metrics - *tops in the industry,*" bragged David.

"What that means to *the client,* is that they won't be listening to music while on hold - wasting their precious time," said Larry converting David's features into benefits. "More importantly, they can get the vast majority of their issues settled in one call and by talking to *one person*. It is the kind of 'white glove' operations service that keeps client's loyal year after year."

"Fantastic! Let's demonstrate service as one of our main competency advantages," remarked Matt. "It also says here that they would be willing to pay a little more in premiums to have a more preferable co-pay structure. *Doesn't that seem a little odd that they would be willing to pay more?*"

"That depends. I assume most of her employed admin staff is younger and beginning to have families," emphasized Larry. "That means they have more visits, thus more co-payments than someone who doesn't need medical services often. Something you will learn soon enough, Matt!"

"Dead on assessment Larry," added Anna, "There were several recent and current pregnancies, including Leanne. I agree that they are feeling the co-pay and deductible pinch."

"That being the case, we have a new product that allows the participant to select a co-pay/deductible design," explained David. "That will give them the flexibility each year to use the plan that helps them budget and plan best for their individual situation."

"Spoken like a *true* trusted advisor," complimented Larry. "David is correct and that new product is industry leading and will put them on the cutting edge of new programs for years to come."

"That was also very important to Leanne as she believed they were behind the times in what they offered," remembered Matt. "I think we have a good foundation for the employees, what about the data for the agents?"

"They have high levels of job satisfaction just like the employees, but they are all over the map in regards to benefit programs," remarked Anna. "Since they are independent contractors and not employees, it will be tough for Mrs. Evans to cover them directly."

"Correct, but there are ways for her to provide them 'access to success' and I think the real value for her with the independents is not in what she can do directly, but providing them avenues to advance within the industry.

"Agreed Matt," began Larry, "We can always approach these agents directly with individual coverage and defined benefit plans. That campaign would be even more successful if Mrs. Evans endorses us. *That is one way* - one which benefits us, but not necessarily the agency. The better approach would be to have the Evans Agency umbrella the agents as they grow - to create a branch development approach."

"That's brilliant!" exclaimed Anna. "The number one request for the independents was an avenue to grow their business from being a single agent to becoming an agency.

Right now, I am guessing that an agent has to leave the Evans Agency to start their own."

"Causing a drop in revenue," said Matt. "No doubt it is her best agents that strike out...taking precious clients and other agents with them. I think we have enough to make a compelling case. *Anyone disagree?*"

"Not me - I think we have a good foundation. The key will be presenting this information in a way that is not negative or hurts their business psyche," said Larry. "We have to lay it out logically and as the next progression in the life of a great business." Anna and David nodded their heads in full agreement.

"Then all that is left is the presentation structure," said Matt. "I will open with an executive summary of our approach, findings and summary recommendation. Then David will outline our 'white glove' treatment and what makes our customer service department 'best in class'. Larry will go next with an outline of specific company programs and benefit designs - *high level only with additional details provided in print.* They have all done this before and we don't want to be too granular at this stage. I will then close with a final summary. Anna, your role will be to keep us on task, record notes and provide technical assists as needed."

"Great outline Matt," reassured Larry. "I have done many of these and for your first time, you have done a great job. In fact, I am beginning to feel confident in our ability to close this account. *Who knows where that will lead?*"

"Yes Matt…great job!" echoed David, "I am glad to be on your team."

Matt felt comfort in their words of support. He also felt confident in the work that had been done and the results that can be expected when "preparation meets opportunity".

The Presentation

F riday morning had come and the team of 4 had congregated in the lobby of the Evans Agency. It was obvious that Matt was nervous as he greeted the group - "Happy Monday everybody! Are you ready for a great meeting?"

"It's Friday," whispered Anna but loud enough for David and Larry to hear all of them laughing.

"It has been such a busy week, the days are running together," he said defensively. "That still begs the question; *are we ready?* Anna, did you check out a projector?"

"Yes, with an extra bulb just in case!"

"It is good that you are nervous Matt. That energy gives you a kick of adrenaline that can be transmuted into high performance enthusiasm," assured Larry. "Just don't go over the top and become Jerry Lewis in the Nutty Professor."

"Jerry Lewis? I thought Eddie Murphy was the Nutty Professor - you know...the Clumps?"

"Please don't go in here with that Generation Y stuff, Mrs. Evans and Mrs. Hicks are more my age," said Larry playfully.

"David, you sure are quiet - *are you ok?*" asked Matt.

"Just going over my lines in my head...I am fine," he said feebly. "No really, I am fine!" he rebutted sensing his first answer was less than convincing.

"This is a small audience of three people and we have our presentation slides and documents to keep us flowing," instructed Larry. "I couldn't think of better people to do this with - you are all more than equipped, skilled and talented for this...*let's go!*"

They headed upstairs and were directed by the receptionist to the boardroom where they could set up. They were finished in minutes and then took seats on various sides of the room. As Leanne, Ms. Hicks and Mrs. Evans entered the room, there was a noticeable chill in the air. A series of cordial but business like introductions did not yield the normal tangential conversations. Matt tested the air for receptivity.

"I hope you had a great trip Mrs. Evans. You certainly got a great tan!"

"Not this time tiger...this is all business. *Your charm is what got you in the door...now you have to dazzle me with brilliance*," she responded for all to hear.

"Certainly, my team and I truly appreciate the opportunity to present a proposal that I believe will be the cornerstone for the next level of growth and opportunity for the Evans Agency. In the next 45 minutes, we will outline that strategy for creating the Evans Agency Happy People Program. It is a program that will set the Evans Agency apart by creating loyal and productive employees and agents in an atmosphere of opportunity for development and personal growth. It is well documented that environments such as these generate increases in revenue, lower costs through efficiencies, and will facilitate organic growth for decades to come - creating a lasting legacy for generations to come." Matt clicks the remote to move to the next slide - It simply says **The American Dream.**

He begins," There is no doubt that the country, the entire world, has gone through great economic changes in the last few years. It has certainly impacted the real estate industry in ways that would have seemed unfathomable a few years prior. However, the Evans Agency has weathered the storm and now has the opportunity to ride the next wave of opportunity. The American Dream has evolved since the chaos of the global meltdown. As people recover and truly evaluate their lives, the dream has gone back to what our forefathers knew prophetically; (clicks to next slide with picture of founding fathers and a quote).

"*We hold these truths to be self-evident, that all men are created equal, that they are endowed by their creator with certain inalienable rights, that among these are Life, Liberty and the Pursuit of Happiness.*" (pause for impact)

"The New American Dream is a return to the *original one*. People now place value in *different places* after watching others, and sometimes themselves, lose the things they once thought of as of primary importance. This is especially evident in the Evans Agency as your employees look for higher work/life satisfaction. How do we know? *...we asked them!*"

(Matt clicks to the next slide entitled **People Love the Evans Agency**!)

"To explain, we conducted a blind survey for all of your employees and 100 independent agents. It was a series of questions primarily designed to ascertain their satisfaction with the company benefits offered. To take it a step further, Mrs. Simpson also had the foresight to include vital questions for workplace satisfaction and career happiness. Yes, these are subjective ideologies, but the survey provides the closest empirical measurements possible." (Matt clicks to the next slide with a series of simple charts showing the various responses. He continues to expound on the common theme of Happy People.)

"Mrs. Evans, you and your team are to be commended as your people, employees and agents alike, *love where they work*. That is the cornerstone of the Evans Agency Happy People Program. Now we need to review a few areas where your people have made it clear they want *more options and opportunity*. The first is in the area of benefit programs. (He clicks to the next slide entitled **Happy People Wish List**)

"Here are a series of survey answers that reflect a wish list from your employees and agents. It is not to say they are *purely dissatisfied*, but indicates areas where more expansive options can better meet their *individual needs*. Most interesting on this slide you will see that your people are actually willing to pay *more for expanded choice* - they aren't even expecting you to do it! In a few moments, Larry will outline our company's industry leading product innovation that answers those desires - the Wish List - *your people* have created. After that, David will outline how we will answer their demand for a better customer service experience from this wish list." (Matt clicks to the final slide entitled **The Evans Agency Family Tree**)

"There is no doubt that the Evans Agency is a family...thus the family tree outlined in this slide. *How do families grow?* The kids get married; have children, and their children have children...all expanding the family base, its reach and power. In the final series of survey results from your people, we have broad consensus from employees and agents alike that they would want *more career opportunities and development* - and do so while remaining a part of the Evans family. You have several members of your staff that would like to transition to a career as an agent. We all know that transition can be difficult but it is vital for their 'pursuit of happiness' that they have a path to follow. Part of being happy is the ability to grow and stretch using their gifts. Same applies to agents who desire to create their own agency. Today, when someone wants to start their own agency, *it is a loss for you* - loss of the agent, clients and the valuable resources of time and energy. We would like to propose an agent and agency development program that keeps it 'all in the family'. (Clicks to next slide)

"To summarize the Wish List action plan created by the survey results;

o Implement innovative cutting edge healthcare products for today's needs of flexibility for growing families.

o Employ modern financial products for today's budgets with an eye on tomorrow goals and dreams.

o Provide a higher level of customer service for enhanced client experience.

o Create a career program for employees and branch agency development for agents.

"To close, the American Dream as delivered by Evans Agency Happy People Program is one that we believe will become best in class and will outshine your contemporaries. You have done the hard part, *the extraordinary part* - you have created a warm, inclusive career focused environment of -"

"*Dare I say it...*Happy People," interjected Mrs. Evans breaking 20 minutes of focused attention and silence. "I follow that Happy People are loyal. That Happy People are more efficient since they have longevity and less turn over for the agency. No doubt that Happy People are vested in their work and the company they work for. Happy people want to take the next logical step in their career - they simply want to *be* Happy. I have to tell you Matt, you *almost* have me convinced...you *almost* have me -"

"*Happy?*" Matt answered. "Wait till you hear from Larry and David and I think you will be ecstatic!"

"I have to check to see if an important call has been returned - let's take a 5 minute break before we begin the next section," instructed Mrs. Evans.

Mrs. Evans, Ms. Hicks left the room and only Leanne from their team remained. She discreetly gave Matt the thumbs up of approval. The others also gave their secret signals of "Great Job!" Matt felt the weight of the moment and knew that there was still work to do, but he hadn't even gotten to the strength of his order with David and Larry. *Yes, it was looking positive and it appeared as if nothing could go wrong.*

Act V - Birth Right

Birth and re-birth of a child

They had returned from a quick break and David was beginning his part of the presentation. At that moment, Matt felt a pulse of vibrations from his phone. It was the special setting he had given Erin when she left him a text message. She *never* sent them when he was at work, so he waited for a discreet moment to look down at his phone.

"It's time!" beckoned the phone.

"*Are you ok?*" asked Larry.

Matt showed him the text and looked around the room as David continued to outline how the company would support the Evans Agency operationally if secured as a client.

"What do I do?" asked Matt.

"You know what to do," said Larry in a reassuring tone, "David and I can handle this."

"Gentlemen, it's not nice to keep secrets," said Mrs. Evans in a serious but impish tone.

"I hate to do this, but I must excuse myself from the rest of the meeting," Matt said timidly. "To explain - *the single most important person in my life is about to give birth to the second most important person...our child.*"

"I guess that would make me third on your list?" said Mrs. Evans slightly annoyed.

"I know there is much at stake here today. When we met at the restaurant, I had no idea of how I would make it in this business - *but I believed.* Now I am in the midst of the single greatest opportunity that could change my life. I also understand that my wife is my precious ruby; the child is a gift from God and the possibility of having you as a client is a privilege - I will understand if leaving jeopardizes that privilege, but I have no choice. Think about this...*one day I will be dropping everything to take care of you!*"

The room was silent and Matt began picking up all his materials and putting them into his briefcase. As he put the final pieces in and prepared to leave, Mrs. Evan's broke the hush that had come over the room.

"My driver will take you to the hospital - you are in no position to drive. I will have him call to have a police escort meet you at the interstate...it will take you less than 20 minutes to get there. *I can't have my new Generational Wealth Specialist getting into an accident.*"

The look on Matt, Larry and David's faces must have shown their surprise at hearing that response.

"Yes, *we can do business*," said Mrs. Evans in a congratulatory voice. "Until this very moment, I didn't know if you were feigning all the virtuous attributes in an effort to get my account. With your willingness to lose this account to be by your wife's side, I have tangibly experienced your sincerity, integrity and honor - the same that I believe you will give this yesterday morning, *and have yet to hear back from him* I just realized that *anyone can sell me products*, but only someone of your character and enthusiasm can give me what I need - the highest level of service and commitment. Now get out of here...Larry and David can take it from here...*right gentlemen?*"

"Of course!" said Larry.

"Yes...get out of here!" supported David.

Matt entered the car with the driver and, as promised, a police motorcycle met them at the on-ramp to the interstate. They pushed past the traffic by driving on the median and in record time, pulled into the admissions area of the hospital. Matt thanked the driver, the saluting policemen and rushed to find Erin. He arrived in the birth staging area out of breath and took Erin's hand.

"You are right on time!" Erin said breathlessly.

"Have I ever let you down?"

"Never!"

The doctor arrived to check her vitals and said in a reassuring tone, "Someone is ready to give birth to a perfect baby. Let's get you back to the birthing table. Young man, *you look nervous.*"

"That's just his look - he can take on the world," said Erin in a matronly tone.

Matt looked on in wonder as the hospital staff was in a flurry of activity. The chaos of the event was supplanted by the seamlessly fluid and orchestrated manner in which the teams did their part and filled their roles. The doctor was the "star" but the other players were no less important. Moreover, they made Erin felt like a princess and the most important person in the world...to Matt, she was both.

There was a crescendo in the hustle and bustle and Matt felt helpless – able only to hold Erin's hand and offering a coach's words of support. Her face was awash with perspiration reminding him of his wheezing early morning runs. With each unrelenting contraction and sporadic command to "push", he wondered if Erin could withstand the physical exertion for much longer. He knew she was exhausted and just at the moment when she looked as if she had given all she could give, the doctor intervened.

"I know it feels as if the baby will never get here, but this precious gift *is imminent*. Take a few breaths of rest and then get ready to give it all you have got...*ok?*"

"Are you ok?" Matt asked wishing he could take her pain.

"I told you, I am stronger than you think. God made me for this...*this is my rite of passage*. Just keep holding my hand and don't let go!"

"Alright princess, it is time to give it your all," commanded the doctor.

The next several moments were filled with staccato bursts as Erin struggled to breathe, explosive grunts as she pushed with all her might and unintelligible words emanating between her screams of pain. The team was oblivious to her sounds, *focused only on the process* and the tasks at hand. Matt on the other hand, felt flush and weak in the knees.

"Father down!" said one of the nurses noticing the look on Matt's face.

"It's just a Vegal Response," said the doctor. "Sit him down right there; get him some juice and a cold towel. Don't worry princess, his response just shows how much he loves you. Stay focused...one more big push ought to do it! That's it...here it comes!"

The next sound Matt heard was the sweetest shrill sound he had ever heard, next to Erin's cooing over the birthstone necklace he had given her at the restaurant. It was the cry of *new life*...exiting the domain and security of the womb and into the unknown environment of a brand new world.

"Here she is...beautiful, perfect *and yours*," announced the doctor placing the squirming bundle on Erin's chest.

"Matt, come and see the most beautiful baby on the world...Natalie Diane Palmer," said Erin breathlessly.

The nurse wheeled the chair that Matt was sitting in next to Erin and everyone left the room to give them a few minutes. He took her by the hand and tried to apologize for his spell. Erin put a wearied finger over his mouth with a gentle "hush" letting him know it wasn't necessary. As he peered over the rail of the bed, he saw a rosy pink baby covered in bits of goo lying peacefully on Erin's chest. She too, was exhausted from the journey. He reached out to take her tiny little hand.

"Daddy's here and everything will be fine," Matt said gathering his strength. In that moment, he felt the tiny hand of infant life constricting softly, barely making it around his pinky. As she held his hand, she yawned from weariness and sweetly drifted off to slumber. He looked up to see that Erin had done the same. *It was only right.* They had stayed the course, in-spite of obstacles, challenges, discomfort of development and the pain of transition; *they had earned their sweet reward of rest.*

Matt allowed himself a few moments to review the momentous events of the day, the last several months and his entire life. He could feel the wisdom of Grandbooty, his father, and LeRoy now inherently becoming a part of his being - *the kind of knowing that comes only from direct experience.* The anxiety and worry he internalized the last few months didn't *change* his destiny; it only made the journey arduous and taxing. His fears now seemed trivial and inconsequential

From this new vantage point of success with the Evan's Agency and the birth of his child, he realized that what appeared to be a random series of events had all orchestrated and conspired to bring him to this moment of achievement, clarity and harmony. He knew that his life would continue to be filled with evolving challenges, but also new opportunity. *He now understood that he has to face it all with the wonder of a child*, unafraid to explore new things, unfazed by falling down when taking new steps and joyous when triumphant - *no matter how small the victory*. It was time to revive, renew and resurrect the dreams of his youth. Just like Grandbooty had relayed how his birth changed *his life*, he now had something bigger than himself to live for. Someone that would always see him as much more than provider, protector, and occasional punisher...Natalie Diane Palmer would call him father!

Birth of a Leader

onday morning Matt was exhausted as he exited the elevator leading to his office. It was almost 8:30am - he just couldn't muster the strength to arrive at his usual time. The weekend had been a whirlwind of activity as a cavalcade of people had come to see Erin and Natalie Diane at the hospital. They would be coming home that evening and the two moms were taking good care of them so Matt decided to go in to tie up a myriad of loose ends. As he turned the corner to his table with the 4 chairs he noticed a bunch of balloons hanging from his chair congratulating him on the new arrival.

"Happy Monday!" chorused Suzy, Brad, David, Larry, and Anna in an effort to surprise him.

"Wow! Happy Monday indeed!" replied Matt.

"How does it feel to be a father?" said Brad the self-professed bachelor.

"Amazing!" She is the most beautiful baby I have ever seen," Matt answered in prerequisite proud father fashion.

"Having children is a game-changer, but a good one," began David. "It truly balances out your life - establishing perspective on what is important in life."

Speaking of which, *you shouldn't be here today!*" admonished Suzy.

"I have so much to do and the moms are taking care of Erin and Natalie Diane who get out of the hospital today after 5pm."

"*What is so important?*" asked Larry, "David and I sealed the deal with the Evan's Agency on Friday. It will be a great account. Anna and my assistant are putting the paperwork together for our review, which we can do *tomorrow*."

"I moved all of your appointments for today to later in the week, working them into your existing schedule," reported Anna. "I also coordinated all the networking and connecting activities you requested last week. People are already in contact with each other and everything is in full motion. I relayed to your clients that you had the baby and that you would be in touch with them on Wednesday. They all extended well wishes. As Larry stated, we are entering the information for the Evans Agency account today. *Is there anything else you need?*"

Matt stood motionless as he realized that he was no longer a producer trying to get his next client, get his paperwork done or make the next call. *He wasn't chief, cook, and bottle washer trying heroically to make it all work.* He was a professional businessman that had systems that worked *for him*.

"I think his silence means you have it all covered," interjected Suzy.

"Yes, Anna, you have done a great job!" complimented Matt. "It is a load off my mind to know the important things are in good hands."

"You have just learned the most important lesson of a leader - *how to delegate*," observed Larry. "Ok father, it is time for some of us to get to work. Take good care of that precious baby...*partner*."

Before Matt could respond, the sales manager came up to Matt and shook his hand in congratulations. "I didn't think I would see you here today," he began. "Now that you are here, I would like you to do me a big favor. I have 20 newbies starting today and would like for you to address them after the sales meeting."

"Me?" Matt asked incredulous.

"You know it is our tradition that the top new sales person provides words of wisdom to the new recruits. With the month you have just had and closing the Evans Agency account, you are #1!"

"You have to be kidding!" Matt said disbelieving. He had never really even thought about the leaderboard beyond his moments of great embarrassment for being at the bottom for so long - certainly, not being at the top of it.

"*What do you say?*" asked the sales manager. "Ok, really you have no choice and after you finish you can leave for the day...agreed?"

"When you put it that way, I guess the answer is yes."

As he walked away Matt turned to Suzy, David and Brad not sure what to express. "I could not have done any of this if not for you guys. I know that we are all running our own individual businesses, but the synergy we have established is a big part of why we will all be successful."

"Don't get all mushy on us," said Brad, "The meeting is about to start."

"*What will I say?*" Matt asked Suzy discreetly.

"Speak the way you *always do*...from the heart and with an unselfish desire to see people succeed."

The meeting was no different than any other and Matt's mind was preoccupied with what he would say. He didn't even notice when the applause was for him being the top new sales person. *So much had happened to get him to that spot.* Now he had the opportunity to impact 20 new people. He didn't even remember who spoke to his group or what they said at his meeting several months ago - *he didn't want that to happen this time.* He only remembered being scared out of his mind in anticipation of the phones and then meeting LeRoy. Now he was here...

"Without further adieu, I am proud to introduce our top new sales person, Matthew Palmer," finished the sales manager.

"Happy Monday everyone!" began Matt. It's great to see so many new faces. It's hard to believe that just a few months ago; I was sitting right where you are. *How do you all feel to be here this morning?* Don't answer that on the grounds it would incriminate you!"

Light laughter filled the room, but it was somewhat awkward. The faces were all smiling but deep down Matt knew they were faces of trepidation.

"Ok, let's be honest with each other. Most of you are scared to death. *How do I know?* Because when I was sitting where you are, I was paralyzed with fear. I was new to sales and had no clue. How many of you are new to sales? (Many hands are raised) As I suspected, the majority of you have *never* done this before. Don't worry, as a good friend once told me, *'most of us fall into sales, but then we fall in love'*. That has happened to me, and it can happen to you. Since I have only a few minutes to relay key words of wisdom on how you will get there, there are 3 things I want to share with you;

#1 - Fear not. As I just admitted, when I was in your shoes, I was terrified. Young wife, baby on the way and 3 months to get it together before the base salary clock ran out. I was so focused on all the things that might go wrong, I couldn't see the solutions that were right in front of me. *I quickly realized that obstacles and struggles are the requirement for progress.* There was really no reason to pay "anxiety interest" on a debt I hadn't incurred. I recently came up with an acronym for FEAR - **Forever Evolving Anticipation of Reality**. Just when you think you have conquered an area, something new will hit you. Each day will be filled with new demands, but simply be prepared to stretch your gifts, talents and most importantly, *your comfort zone*. Each day get a little better and I promise the fear will lessen and in time you will meet each evolving challenge with courage and faith.

#2 - Find your voice. All of you have just gone through the two-week Fast Start Training and today you will begin work on the phones. Not to steal the sales managers thunder, but *'the phone is your friend!'* It is an opportunity to use the *one thing* that is natural to you even in this foreign environment - *your voice*. Not just the voice that speaks words to convince someone to meet with you or buy your product, but the voice that conveys sincerity, integrity and the unique experiences that make up who you are. Larry Wilcox, the company's top producer, and my partner, says that *you* are The Messenger. The *product* is The Message. To be most productive, you have to engage your *authentic voice* - that is the one that people will respond to. How do you know when you are using that voice? *Things just feel right*. When you begin to sound like you are copying or imitating others, you are outside of your voice. People will sense you are pressing the issue and it will shut down the sale. Speak professionally, but be true to your essence and who you are as a human being...*the inherent human connections will build the bridge to sales*.

#3 - Seek help. I stand before you today an accomplished man - *#1 in fact*. Suave, debonair and charismatic - virtues that I am certain you have already picked up on! Don't let the charm and good looks fool you...I didn't get this way on my own. Just a few days into the phones, *I was dead last on the* *leaderboard and on the verge of being fired.* I swallowed my pride and sought help. It came in the form of an unlikely mentor. He blessed me with 30 days that help turned my situation around. I also enlisted the help of a like-minded group of colleagues, the sales manager and the top gun. Before you all go running to Larry, realize that you have to demonstrate you are willing to put in the effort and energy to be worthy of mentorship - *he is rightfully tough on people who only want an easy way.* My door is open to help but <u>no one</u> can make it easy. The company has given you 'access to success" and you have to engage persistence and ingenuity to make the most of it - *the tools are all there but get help when you need it.*

The last thing I would tell you is to have fun and enjoy the journey. As I have learned in my short time here, the small things bring the best results and happiness. *I have learned to feast on the crumbs* - not waiting on the next big deal, but relishing the small ones and everything in-between. The next several months and years will be filled with many 'firsts', but *what other career can give you Emancipation, Gratification and great Remuneration?* Be free, be grateful and make lots of money. *Welcome to the club of professional sellers - do our industry proud!"*

Matt went to the back of the room and one by one, the newbies stood to their feet applauding the lessons in truth they had just received. *Their reaction was spontaneous and genuine.* He had not delivered "pie in the sky" optimism or blatant motivational brainwashing. He had poured out the essence of the last three months of his life. As they continued to show their thanks, his colleagues and friends gathered around him to show support.

"I guess we can add inspirational speaker to your growing list of talents," said David. "You have certainly been an inspiration to me...I owe you a lot...thank you!"

"I am honored to know you and one day, I will be able to say I knew you way back when!" added Brad. "Of course, by then, I will be CEO!"

"Now that is the Matt I knew would emerge," said Suzy proudly as she hugged him warmly. "*Wonderfully perfect...perfectly wonderful!*"

"Thank you all for being so supportive, motivating and there to help me through the challenges," said Matt sincerely. "As the preacher said yesterday, '*We have fought the good fight*' and now it is time to feast on the spoils. The best part of this journey is *ahead* of us...I look forward to our success and continued friendship."

As he was heading out of the office, one of the new recruits walked up to him. "Mr. Palmer, my name is Jeffrey Townes and I just wanted to tell you how inspired I was by what you said. *Much of what you described is my story.* I am eager but fighting fear just like you said. I even had to work up the nerve to come and ask if you could give me some additional words of wisdom over lunch one day...*my treat.*"

"Well Jeffrey, your first lesson - *'a man that is willing to invest in his success will surely have some'.* How does next Monday after the sales meeting sound?"

"That sounds great - whew...*I feel better already*!" Jeffrey relayed with unabashed excitement.

As Jeffrey walked off to get started on *his journey*, Matt opened the door to begin the next leg of his - one filled with fatherhood, a wonderful wife, a loving family *and now a career that he knew would provide for them.* As he said a quiet prayer of success for Jeffrey, his heart was full of gratitude as he thought about how his life had progressed - how everything and everyone was connected - needing each other for a season. His eyes filled with tears of appreciation for a great life...a blessed life. All he could say softly to himself...

"So do I Jeffrey....*so do I.*"

Epilogue - A final crumb

T he next week's Monday morning sales meeting was about to begin and life was almost back to normal, albeit *very busy* - the new normal for Matt. LeRoy was also scheduled to be back in the office and Matt was excited to get to see him and tell him all that had happened while he was gone. The Sales VP was back in the office and Matt wondered what could be happening *this time*. He then notices that he and LeRoy are shaking hands. The VP then stood at the front of the room and addressed the team. He informed the team that LeRoy was officially retiring after 30 years of faithful and productive service. There was even a letter from the company president! Matt went to LeRoy after the obligatory well wishes from people who had never taken the time to get to know him.

"Why didn't you tell me?" Matt asked working hard to keep hold of his emotions.

"I didn't know until after our last lunch," began LeRoy also holding *his emotions* at bay. "I will still service my faithful clients, but have decided to relax and enjoy my family more - travel and a life of leisure. Before I could sail into that sunset, I had to have a confirmation and an assurance that there would be at least *one* person here who could carry on my mission and do it with a high degree of integrity and professionalism. *That person is you.* I thank you for allowing me to be a small part of your life. A Crumb..."

Matt finishes the statement, "*From the Master's Table.*" Matt couldn't believe it was all happening so fast. "Can we keep up with each other...maybe over lunch?"

"Of course, a man should never work on an empty stomach! Remember all that I have taught you, and remember, no matter what - *your mission!* I have great faith in you and have full assurance that you will accomplish everything you set your hand to do. God Bless!"

They shook hands warmly and shared a manly embrace. With no fanfare or gold watch, LeRoy left as anonymously as he had worked the past three decades. Matt felt a little empty as he watched him leave but knew he was right. He had just been handed the baton and had to live up to the promise.

A sense of urgency and eagerness filled his heart and mind as he moved to occupy his seat at the table with 4 phones - which quickly turned into a cube, and within a year as he garnered "rookie of the year" turned into a small office. Within 3 years, Matt was moved to a private office with Anna as his company provided assistant. By his 5th year, he was the first person to be top producer 12 months in a row, where he appropriately had the words 'top producer' changed to 'top cultivator'. Throughout, he was always willing to lend quick advice to the newbies, never forgetting how he had gotten started, but remained focused on the mission he had established with LeRoy at the cafe, *and the lessons that life had taught him about sales and life mastery.*

He and LeRoy kept in touch as promised. They had lunch every month to begin with, but as with all things, life's demands necessitated the meetings become quarterly, and with the passing of years, a much anticipated annual reunion. *A full decade after Leroy's retirement, Matt was now quite successful.* He and his wife Erin were expecting their third child, they just purchased a magnificent home at the country club and every dream they had dreamed was a reality. Of course, he still had his mission and remained focused on it. There had been the opportunities for promotion, but Matt remained true to his calling, knowing it was his "highest and best" use for this stage of his life.

Matt was preparing for the now annual luncheon with LeRoy and he was especially excited to share news of all the happenings of the past year. As he arrived at the cafe, he immediately noticed their usual location was unoccupied. That's odd; LeRoy was always 15 minutes early *wherever* he was going. Matt took his seat and looked around for the cafe owner. He called a familiar face to the table to inquire, "Is the owner here today?"

"No, he will be back shortly," he answered

"I am also looking for LeRoy, my friend, who has come here for many years sitting right in this very spot."

"Oh yes, *the insurance salesman*," answered the waiter.

He must not have known LeRoy with *that* description chuckled Matt thinking to himself. "Yes, that is him."

Just then the cafe owner walks up and greets Matt with a hearty welcome. "Here sits Matthew Palmer, Generational Wealth Specialist," he said like he was announcing royalty. "Mr. LeRoy wanted me to give you this letter and beg forgiveness."

"*Is he ok?*" Matt asked in a worried voice.

"No need to worry, my friend, he is doing fine. Read the letter and all will be explained."

He looked at the envelope and his name, Matthew Palmer was there and underneath it simply said, *One Last Crumb*. As Matt opened the handwritten letter, he got nervous wondering what it could be. The letter was on beautiful parchment paper and written in LeRoy's own handwriting. It began;

Dearest Matthew,

I will be brief as all the important things were said between us 10 years ago over a magical 30 day period. While you credit me with teaching, it was you that taught me more. You taught me that I have a new mission...one of mentorship for others like you. That is why I am going back home to teach others what I know and raise another generation of professional sellers. Thank you for listening to an old man who was filled with age old wisdom.

One more thing, now that I have officially fully retired to my new calling, I need someone to look after my friends who have entrusted their lives to me over the years. Here is a letter I sent to all of my clients;

My friends,

I thank you for allowing me to play a small part in your lives and the lives of those you love. As I transition into another phase of life, I want to introduce you to my kindred spirit - Matthew "Matt" Palmer. He is worthy of your trust and will assist you as I did with a genuine heart and love of service. Please open your lives to him as you did for me.

Health, happiness, and a lot of money!

Conrod Athelstan LeRoy Shuffler

What did it all mean? The cafe owner came over and saw the perplexed look on Matt's face. "What troubles you?" he asks, "Mr. LeRoy has just left you the keys to the Kingdom!"

"What do you mean?"

"As I understand it, Mr. LeRoy just turned over his book of business, his clients, *to you*. You were indeed fortunate to have LeRoy take such interest in you; he is truly a great man! He came to me 40 years ago with this notion of helping me Eradicate Poverty. His wisdom and persistence are the reason I opened my first cafe and subsequently, guided me to start or purchase over 10 businesses - all that have been very successful. I owe him my life. *That is why I would never allow him to pay for lunch.*"

"Pardon me, you mean LeRoy *never* paid for lunch?" Matt asked pretending to be perturbed.

"Not in over 40 years, even though the meal was free for him and his guest - *and he always left a generous $10 tip!* That is the kind of man he is."

Matt burst out into spontaneous laughter. LeRoy was certainly one of a kind. *Now he realizes he could have eaten too!!!*

The cafe owner continued with more revelation, "It might surprise you to know, that he is very wealthy and is very generous to his family and community. As a man who started with nothing, coming to this country with $200 in his wife Pamela's shoe, he rose to heights of greatness in his chosen profession, creating a financial and spiritual legacy for generations to come." Matt was shocked to hear all of this about LeRoy, in over a decade, he *never* said a word of his achievements.

The cafe owner, realizing he had surprised the young man said, "Enough of my going on, you are here, please have lunch – you are now the benefactor of LeRoy's complimentary lifetime of lunches. *The special perhaps? Can I interest you in bread?*"

"You can always interest me in bread, warm with butter please - *In honor of my good friend.*"

As the bread arrived a small group of birds circled close. As Matt finished the crusty roll, he did as he had seen LeRoy do many times. He carefully scraped all the crumbs into his palm and extended the hand of generosity to the gathering flock. To his surprise, the first bird, the second, third and fourth bird gently came to take the offering. As he contemplated the last 10 years and all that has transpired, he has a deeper understanding life of life; *A new revelation that was borne out of his years of struggle, hope and success - an irreplaceable wealth of experiences that forged who he was at this moment.* As tears emerged and streamed down his face, his heart danced in unison with the jubilant birds enjoying *their* divine provision. Witnessing this scene afresh, he recalls the question from LeRoy from the first day they met. He looks up into the pristine blue sky and says without reservation and out loud for all to hear...

"Yes, LeRoy, *I believe it.*"

About Brandon L. Clay

Brandon L. Clay is an author/story-teller, international speaker, and sales leader. For the past 28 years, he has delivered his distinctive brand of instruction and inspiration to over 30,000 sales professionals and 1,000's of others outside the sales arena. His strength is that he understands that there is no standardized template or "cookie cutter" approach to creating high sales achievers. His power of connection allows him to recognize and leverage each person's unique talents and help them unleash their greatest potential.

In February 2011, inspired by his father-in-law, LeRoy Shuffler, and combined with his experience of the 1,000's of people touched and transformed by his unique combination of life and sales mastery, he penned **Sales Crumbs from the Master's Table.** Brandon's entertaining, empowering, and enlightening approach to coaching sales excellence is brought to life through this simple story. It quickly become regarded as a *must read* for anyone in sales and inspired the follow-up volumes in the Trilogy - **A Trail of Sales Crumbs** and **Feasting On Sales Crumbs**. This trilogy is now touching everyone from CEO's, VP's, managers, seasoned veterans, to "newbies" in their first week and helping him fulfill his mission of Helping Millions Achieve Success...One At A Time.

He lives in McDonough, Georgia with his high school sweetheart, Natalie, and their 3 children, Chaz, Christian, and Faith.

Learn more about Brandon, his available programs and additional resources at

www.brandonlclay.com

Additional Titles Available from Brandon L Clay;

<u>Sales Crumbs Trilogy</u>
Volume I - Sales Crumbs from the Master's Table
Volume II - A Trail of Sales Crumbs
Volume III - Feasting On Sales Crumbs

Your Authentic Sales Voice - *Discovering and unleashing your most natural gift for greater sales success!*

The Power to Change - *7 Day Life Transformation Guide*
S = ME²- *Revolutionary Success Formula!*

The 80% Sales Solution - *Training program based on the popular Sales Crumbs Trilogy*